THE INTERN FILES

HOW TO GET, KEEP, AND MAKE THE
MOST OF YOUR INTERNSHIP

BY JAMIE FEDORKO

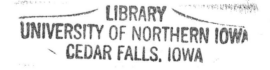

SSE

SIMON SPOTLIGHT ENTERTAINMENT

NEW YORK   LONDON   TORONTO   SYDNEY

SSE

SIMON SPOTLIGHT ENTERTAINMENT

An imprint of Simon & Schuster

1230 Avenue of the Americas, New York, New York 10020

Text copyright © 2006 by Jamie Fedorko

Illustrations copyright © 2006 by Dwight Allott

All rights reserved, including the right of reproduction in whole or in part in any form.

SIMON SPOTLIGHT ENTERTAINMENT and related logo are trademarks of

Simon & Schuster, Inc.

Designed by Yaffa Jaskoll

Manufactured in the United States of America

First Edition   10   9   8   7   6   5   4   3   2   1

Library of Congress Cataloging-in-Publication Data

Fedorko, Jamie.

The intern files : how to get, keep, and make the most of your internship /

by Jamie Fedorko.—1st ed.

p. cm.

ISBN-13: 978-1-4169-0921-7

ISBN-10: 1-4169-0921-4

1. Internship programs. 2. Interns. I. Title.

LC1072.I58F43 2006

378.3'65—dc22

2005029904

CONTENTS

ACKNOWLEDGMENTS   v

INTRODUCTION: There's No Such Thing as an Entry-Level Position:
Welcome to the Wonderful World of Internships   vii

PART I: GETTING THE INTERNSHIP
Chapter 1: Career Choices   3
Chapter 2: The Résumé and Cover Letter (with Alexis Feldman)   7
Chapter 3: Find Your School's Internship Director   15
Chapter 4: Applying for Internships   21
Chapter 5: The Interview (with Alexis Feldman)   31
Chapter 6: The Interviews Are Over. Now What?   41

PART II: THE FIRST DAY
Chapter 7: What to Wear   49
Chapter 8: The First Day, Part I   57
Chapter 9: The Chain of Command   61
Chapter 10: Seek Out Your Fellow Interns   67
Chapter 11: The First Day, Part II   71

PART III: HOW TO BE THE PERFECT INTERN
Chapter 12: Make Yourself Known   79
Chapter 13: Get It Done   85

Chapter 14: There's Never Nothing to Do   91
Chapter 15: Don't Get Taken Advantage Of   97
Chapter 16: Super Intern to the Rescue!   107

PART IV: SOCIAL ETIQUETTE AT THE OFFICE
Chapter 17: Do Your Work, Then Tell
    Suzie About Your Weekend   115
Chapter 18: Who to Befriend   121
Chapter 19: How to Handle Work Functions   131
Chapter 20: Networking   133
Chapter 21: Sex   135

PART V: THE BEGINNING OF THE END
Chapter 22: Winding Down   147
Chapter 23: Self-Evaluation/Exit Interview   153
Chapter 24: What If You Hated It?   159
Chapter 25: The Letter of Recommendation   163
Chapter 26: Job Opportunities   167

CONCLUSION   173

APPENDIX   185

ACKNOWLEDGMENTS

First, to the people who have made this book possible from the beginning and have seen it through to the end: everyone at Simon Spotlight Entertainment and Trident Media. I thank you for your support, your guidance, and most of all, for putting up with me throughout the writing process.

Danielle Shingleton and Diane Drennan from my time at *Paper* magazine: Thank you for giving me the chance to really show what I was capable of when no one else did: I can't say that this book would exist without you.

Also, Andrew Simon from my time at *VIBE* magazine, and the staff at *The McEnroe Show*: Thank you for all the knowledge and experience I was able to obtain through you.

This book, however, along with the careers of hundreds upon thousands of young adults, would not have been possible without the wisdom of Renée Alexander, a former internship director at Eugene Lang College at the New School University. Your seemingly endless passion for helping students discover and reach their goals, whatever they may be, does not go unnoticed. Trust me when I say that I speak for students past, present, and future: Without you, there probably would be hundreds of us walking around wondering what the hell to do with our lives. You gave—and I'm sure will continue to give—us direction when before all we had were ideas, hopes, and dreams. I cannot thank you enough.

Andrea Serkin and Alexis Feldman: You certainly fall into the next category, but I also thank you for your contributions.

And lastly, my close friends and family. I'm lucky enough to say that you know who you are, so I needn't waste time on names, but I will say that if a man is judged by the company he keeps, then because of all of you, I am forever in good standing. How you've tolerated me over the years I'm not sure, but thanks, and keep up the good work: We've got a long way to go!

THERE'S NO SUCH THING AS AN ENTRY-LEVEL POSITION: WELCOME TO THE WONDERFUL WORLD OF INTERNSHIPS

 "INTERNSHIP." THE WORD ON ITS OWN SOUNDS SO DAMN IMPORTANT, DOESN'T IT? ALMOST SOUNDS LIKE AN APPRENTICESHIP OF SOME SORT— something great, something meaningful, and most of all, something that says "power." Well, outside of their potential to give potential to a potential career, internships aren't exactly glamorous.

As an intern, you likely won't see a dime, and your name probably won't be attached to any important document or company account, but it's not quite as bad as it sounds. In fact, whether or not you do end up working on something terribly important, interning while you're in college allows you the chance to make important career decisions without the real-world risks. You can begin to try your hand at fields that interest you, and by the time you graduate, you'll probably have a great sense of what it is you want to do in your career. It may take you ten years without an internship to discover what you'll learn in three weeks while interning, and that is invaluable.

This book will diagram a step-by-step plan for you. You'll figure out exactly how to begin the process of interning, both from the school end and from the work end, and then you'll understand what to do when you get there: how to act, what to say, what to wear, and how to balance school and interning, while still maintaining a social life. *The Intern Files* will even guide you through the end of an internship and will explain how to parlay a once unpaid, hapless gig into a barely paid, mildly appreciated entry-level job.

As wonderful as the experience can be, it's not all fun and games. In fact, many interns feel uncomfortable at their first internships. This book will help you transform yourself from couch-potato college kid into high-powered Super Intern. Trust me.

While you may feel powerless right now, whether you're looking for an internship or even if you have one, the internship has actually become an important step toward being gainfully employed. And while it may feel like all it means is long hours, no or low pay, and extreme attitude from everyone above you, by interning while in college—or even sooner—you may save yourself from some bottom-feeding when you do enter the real world. You'll be able to walk into interviews with confidence about your experience in the workplace. Your résumé will resonate with talent and labor. Your references will gush about you, and the steadiness in your voice will distinguish you from other potential hires . . . if you worked as hard as you possibly could at your internships. If you didn't . . . good luck!

While you probably won't get paid as an intern, and you don't command any respect, the good news is that no one will expect anything more than utter stupidity from you. So most people are actually going to be astonished by anything you do right, no matter how minor or menial the task. It's not about *you*, it's just that expectations for interns are universally low. And that's a good thing. This book will tell you how to impress people, and how to garner the respect that any hard-working intern deserves.

And you've got this on your side: Companies are relying on interns more and more these days. Though they might treat you like a rodent, they need you! Interns who begin to stick out from the crowd can easily become a part of a company's backbone. Of course, you'll do some mundane tasks, too—those things are absolutely necessary. But interns have no ceiling. You can make your internship whatever you want it to be, and by guiding you through the key steps to becoming a valuable intern and sharing true experiences with you, this book will help optimize the experience.

You might be asking yourself, "Why do I want an internship again?" Yeah, it sounds like more work than play, but if you do want to make something of yourself, as many a grandfather has probably suggested that you do, it's going to be incredibly challenging, if not impossible, to do so without internship experience. So unless you want to reside in the mailroom for years on end, you've got to subject yourself to a small dose of conformity—part of which is interning. And remember, interning is not an event, but an experience that will benefit you down the road, and thus it requires great patience.

Once you have had a good internship, you'll probably find that it was one of the most rewarding and enjoyable experiences of your life. You're only a few years away from the start of your adult life—the life that involves *you* paying the bills, that is. Interning means getting to spend a few days a week participating in an up-close, live version of *The*

Real World: Work Life, and that is something that shouldn't be taken for granted.

Being an intern is like taking a test drive, only you're both the car and the driver. Companies get to test you, you get to test entire fields, and there's very little to be lost, but so much to be gained. You have the ability to do as much or as little as you want as an intern: the ability to begin to carve out a finely etched drawing of your future. Or you can just watch others do what you hope to do after college while you half-ass it the whole time. Either way, you can really make the experience as wonderful or as terrible as you want to—it's all up to you.

This book will illuminate methods you can follow to get, keep, and make the absolute most of every moment of your internships. Hopefully, it also shows you why it is not only important, but not so bad, to work before you technically have to. If all goes well, you should learn how to work hard and enjoy it by the time you've finished this book. Okay, it's weird to see "work" and "enjoy" in the same sentence. But believe it or not, once you find your niche, you'll love getting up and going to work, even if there's not a paycheck with your name on it. If you pay close enough attention to what you're about to read, you'll probably learn a bit about yourself and what you want to do with your career.

And lastly, there's even solace if you're concerned with not getting paid. Here's my theory: The worst part of interning (you know, not getting paid) may be, in retrospect, the biggest blessing in disguise in the entire world. By working for free or for credit, by being a person who is taken seriously only once you have proven yourself, you are free. Free to push yourself to the limit in terms of how hard you are willing to work. Free to not work so hard and find out what the consequences are really like. Free to explore the career world with wonderment and a ceiling so high it's nearly impossible to see with the naked eye.

Use this idea of freedom as a method of empowerment every time you don't feel like going to your internship. Hold tight to the belief that you are not only lucky, but also truly blessed in your intern skin, and the whole experience should open up more doors for you, both personally and professionally, than you ever imagined.

Just keep this in mind: Companies are searching for, and will generally hire, the intern who falls directly in between the two standard types. First, there is the know-it-all, arrogant, "I don't really have to be here" kind of intern. Then there is the overbearing, unconfident, "please let me scrub your toilet" kind of intern. Companies are searching for the happy medium: interns who will do anything, and do it with confidence and grace. Interns who understand why they are where they are, but also exude an "I *want* to be here" kind of attitude every day. The ideal intern, which you'll know exactly how to become once you've read *The Intern Files*, is a young man or woman who is confident, but unafraid to ask questions. Someone who doesn't need a babysitter while on an errand or answering the phone. Someone who may not be able to drink legally, but who is still secure in his or her ability to learn and grow professionally and as a human being.

At the end of the day, you can either be a participant or an innocent bystander. Through stories collected from real-life interns, this book will show you what happens to those who do it the right way, and what happens to those who think interning is a right or a joke. In reality, interning is a privilege and should be taken seriously, but it should also be a damn good time.

In addition to getting real-life stories from former interns, I've spoken with Diane Drennan, an internship coordinator at *Paper* magazine, and Renée Alexander, a former internship director at Eugene Lang College, for their expert advice.

FROM THE INTERN FILES OF THE INTERNSHIP COORDINATOR

The ideal intern, believe it or not, doesn't always have to be the most experienced one. A positive attitude and a willingness to assist on any and all projects is a bonus and can make an intern a valuable asset to a team. An ideal intern should not be afraid to ask questions when they do not understand instructions or if they become confused on a project. Nothing is worse than an intern completing a project the wrong way when asking a simple question would have avoided the entire situation. It doesn't hurt if you can think on your feet and be an effective problem solver. Make yourself indispensable to the staff and you will be awarded better projects.

WHO'S WHO?

Internship coordinator: Is in charge of hiring and overseeing all interns at a particular company.

Internship supervisor: The person who is in direct supervision of you on the job.

Internship director: Runs your school's internship program.

Internship advisor: While the internship director runs the program, you may have a separate advisor as well.

PART I | GETTING THE INTERNSHIP

IF YOU'RE THE TYPICAL NINETEEN- OR TWENTY-YEAR-OLD, YOU PROBABLY HAVE A VAGUE IDEA OF WHAT YOU WANT TO DO, BUT YOU'RE NOT QUITE SURE.
Right? Right.[1] In all likelihood, you have more than one passion, which makes it that much harder to decide where to start.

Companies do exist that bring all of your passions together, but it's possible they don't offer internships, or aren't located in your area. Don't put all your eggs in one internship basket—make sure you have options and a plan of attack. Let's say your lifelong dream is to play second base for the Cubs, headline a major stadium tour with twenty other famous bands, and run a Fortune 500 company, all at the same time. Well, take things step by step. Perhaps seek your first internship with an organization that deals with major league baseball. Then, for your next internship, look for a company that handles some of your favorite rock bands, and for your third internship, try to work at a financial group that will

---

1. Those of you who think you know exactly what to do, good luck, and we'll see you in the career counseling office in four years. Just kidding! You'll make a fine rapper.

tie all your passion and your pragmatism into one tightly laced knot.

There are a lot of resources to use to figure out what industry you want to intern in, but nobody will know what you want to do as well as you do. This means exploration. Dig deep into the six-year-old in you and remember what it is that you love. Even though college should be about figuring out what you want, a lot of students are just doing what they think they're supposed to do, or what their parents told them to do. Interning should be a way to channel the real you. Whether the real you is a fledgling rock star or a future power broker, you won't be able to figure these things out without experience. Don't forget, you're on a test drive—you have absolutely nothing to lose.

FROM THE INTERN FILES OF THE INTERNSHIP DIRECTOR

One of the most positive outcomes of an internship is career clarification: This is what I do want to do. This is what I don't want to do. Imagine wanting to work in publishing, being an excellent writer, taking courses, having fabulous grades, graduating, starting a career in publishing, and being miserable. It happens. Career clarification is not to be overlooked.

There are three ways to choose a field:

1. Follow your passion.
2. Follow your major, which might be your passion.
3. Choose blindly in an attempt to pad your résumé (not recommended!).

No matter how you decide on a field for your internship, don't worry. You can try your hand at many things—you don't have to make every vital career decision by the end of the year.

Many schools have ways to incorporate your internship credits into your major. So if you're majoring in art history, you might want to look for an internship at a museum. If you're a business major who's always wanted to work in the record industry, apply for an internship at a local record company or radio station. You'll gain tangible experience in a field you love, and get some credits, too.

Deciding on a career is a daunting task. Try to combine pragmatism with passion. You do have a lot of freedom, so it's best to begin by trying your hand at something that you *want* to do, rather than something you feel you *have* to do.[2]

---

2. If that's the rule, the exception is for people who are determined to do one thing and one thing only: make money. If that's your goal, simply follow the trail you think leads to the fattest wallet.

"I *THOUGHT* I KNEW WHAT I WANTED WHEN I WAS NINETEEN.... THANK GOD FOR INTERNSHIPS!" —KELLY

I was attending college in New York City and thought that I wanted to work in TV—you know, something glamorous, sexy, and hip. Well, I managed to land a couple of really high-powered internships, and I also got hired right out of college at a job any recent grad would have been thrilled to get.

However, the TV world took its toll on me: It was shallow, low paying, low powered, and highly stressful. Well, most jobs are stressful, but I learned quickly that the stress is only worth it when you're either really dedicated to a job, or it's paying you enough that seeing that check justifies the stress! In my case, however, the bills weren't paying themselves, and I felt damn near empty.

I wasn't working on anything I believed in, and I wasn't doing anything for anyone else, either. I felt like I had put all this time and hard work into my internships; how could it all be for naught? Then one day it hit me: It wasn't all for nothing. My hard work had paid off in a way that I may never have expected. I learned, after three internships and a few real gigs after college, that TV was the last place I wanted to be. THANK YOU, INTERNSHIPS!

If I hadn't interned, I probably would have spent years doing odd jobs while I tried to break into TV, where I'd eventually learn exactly what I've just now discovered: that I hate it! Now I'm working at a dance studio, and although I can't say I'm sure of my future, I can guarantee you it will be far from the small screen. The difference is, I'm only twenty-five—had I not interned, I might have learned this when I was thirty!

THE RÉSUMÉ AND COVER LETTER
(WITH ALEXIS FELDMAN)

 CREATING THE PERFECT RÉSUMÉ CAN SEEM IMPOS-SIBLE. IT'S NOT. WHILE YOU DO NEED TO WORRY ABOUT FORMAT, CONTENT, WORD COUNT, AND PRESENTATION, calm down. Here are a few tips to ease your mind and guide you through the process.

TIP #1: RELAX, THERE IS NO SUCH THING AS THE "PERFECT" RÉSUMÉ

If there were such a thing as the perfect, ultimate résumé, then you wouldn't see countless books and Web sites dedicated to them. There would be one book and one Web site, each saying, "Here. This is it." That is not the case. There are many different formats, and one is not necessarily better than the next. The rules aren't set in stone, so keep that in mind when you're having an anxiety attack over the font size of your name or the spacing between your address and education.

TIP #2: THE MORE THE MERRIER

Before you worry about the content, look at the presentation. Don't listen to the old adage your mother probably told you a hundred times growing up, "Don't judge a book by its cover." She was wrong. Appearance counts. To create your ideal résumé, you should look at as many examples as you can get your hands on. With the invention of the Internet, this task has become much simpler. You can buy the books or look at the Web sites; either way, critiquing various résumés is the easiest way to separate what you like from what you don't like. Ask some friends if you can see their résumés too; these are great resources because you know the authors personally and can see how they make themselves look good. And check with your career counseling office at school—some colleges help with résumé writing by offering seminars or one-on-one tutorials. Why not check them out? Worst-case scenario: You learn what you do not want your résumé to look like.

TIP #3: DON'T GET BOGGED DOWN BY THE WORDING

After you have completed your research and acquainted yourself with the résumé-writing world, it's time for some writing of your own. This doesn't mean organizing your contact information or educational background. Get a pen and paper and start writing down jobs you have held in the past that you plan on using for your résumé.

This is the time to organize your thoughts and simplify the writing process. Think of it as your working outline. List all the résumé-appropriate jobs you've held (this means the work experience that will be useful at the job you are applying for; leave off your semilegal positions).

For each job, you should note five things: job title, company/organization you worked for, dates and location of employment, and responsibilities. The first four are simple; they don't require much thought. The fifth, however, is where you need to focus most of your time. Remember, this is an outline, so don't fret over wording or content. Write down as many of your day-to-day work tasks—and larger assignments—as you can remember. Once you have done so for all your jobs, you are ready for the next step.

TIP #4: SOUND PROFESSIONAL, EVEN IF YOU'RE NOT YET A PROFESSIONAL

Now that you've laid the groundwork, you must organize. Make every task you include in your responsibilities section sound important—even if it wasn't. Use action verbs, and refer to other résumés for helpful wording. For example, instead of writing, "Responsible for faxing, picking up phones," try, "Responsible for interoffice communication." Sounds way more important, right? Try to express the simplest office tasks in the most impressive way. Don't get too caught up with this and make photocopying seem like brain surgery. But find ways to make the most mundane tasks sound important.

Most companies ask for your résumé and cover letter before they agree to interview you, so both documents need to represent you positively and do the speaking for you.

It's sad but true: Image is everything. You make yourself look good by making sure the writing in your résumé is sound, your spelling and grammar are spotless, and the format is perfect (things like spacing, punctuation, and underlining are used in the same manner throughout).

Résumés are the deciding factor between getting an interview and getting absolutely nothing. They are the first way you present yourself to the person who will interview you.

THE PERFECT RÉSUMÉ

Jonathan Internstein
555 Fordham Street, Apt. 3
New York, NY 00000
(212) 555-0013
jinternstein@fordham.edu

EDUCATION:

Fordham University at Lincoln Center, New York, NY
Bachelor of Arts: Expected Graduation Date, May 2006
Double Major: English and Political Science
GPA: 3.56

Trinity College Dublin, Dublin, Ireland
Junior Year Abroad: 2004–2005
Double Major: English and Political Science

AWARDS AND HONORS:
- Dean's Scholarship
- Mississippi Governor's School Scholar Class of 2001
- National Honor Society Member 2000–2001, 2001–2002

EXPERIENCE:

8/03–8/04 **The Outback Steakhouse**, New York, NY
Host
- Greeted guests and controlled the flow of tables in the restaurant
- Took orders over the telephone and organized orders to send out for delivery

3/03–5/03 **Fordham Admissions Office**, New York, NY
Telecounselor
- Contacted prospective students about admission procedures and handled all inquiries
- Aided in updating the database of prospective students

9/02–2/03 **Beacher's Comedy/Comedy Gone Wild**, New York, NY
Promotions Intern
- Responsible for promotion of biweekly shows and events
- Visited local colleges and universities and other spots around the city to promote upcoming events
- Oversaw seating at events and helped make sure things ran smoothly

ACTIVITIES:
- *Editor*, **Trinity College's Sociology and Political Science Review**, 2004–2005
- *Freshman Senator*, **Student Government**, 2002–2004
- *Volunteer*, **Annual Star Breakfast**, December 2002
- *Member*, **Fordham University's Pre-Law Society**, 2003–2004
- *Kaplan Campus Representative*, **Fordham University at Lincoln Center**, 2003–2004

After you're satisfied with your résumé (at least for now—remember, you can revise it at any time), the next order of business is your cover letter. In a nutshell, this brief letter should express three things: your interest in working for a company, the reason you are interested in the position, and your appreciation for the company taking the time to review your résumé and (hopefully) speak with you further. This letter is read before your résumé, so its main purpose is to entice the HR department or internship coordinator to learn more about you. It's only a paragraph long, so you have just a few sentences to make yourself sound incredible—to both sell yourself and keep the reader interested enough to move on to your résumé.

While addressing those three points in your letter, keep in mind that this is a way to grab the reader's attention. You want them to think, "This is impressive, I have to take a look at this kid's résumé." To your potential employers, you are just another applicant. But if you come across as intelligent and slightly more interesting than the last candidate, you're pushing yourself toward the top of the pile. In every interaction or communication, you have to remember that you are selling yourself.

It's a dog-eat-dog world out there. You have one chance to get this internship, so pull out all the stops. Try to sound like yourself, but don't come across like a show-off. Keep your letter professional while also maintaining a sense of "you." Don't sound robotic or contrived. They're hiring a person, not a machine.

It sounds overwhelming, but you'll find that there are tons of people, books, and Web sites that can help you write a strong cover letter and résumé. Check out the cover letter on the next page for inspiration.

November 15, 2006

Bill Moldoun
Internship Coordinator
Perfect Medical Company
Companytown, NY 11111

Dear Mr. Moldoun:

I'm writing to you regarding the available internship at your company next fall. I'm a communications major at Atlanta University, minoring in sociology, and have a very strong interest in helping and communicating with people, particularly in the medical field. I feel that my prior experience working part-time at a hospital while in high school will benefit me greatly as an intern at your company. I've seen patients in need firsthand and would love to learn the business side of providing people with the insurance they need. Also, studying communications and sociology has instilled in me a great understanding of and willingness to work with people in need under any circumstance. I'm a fast learner and a patient student, and I work extremely well under pressure.

Thank you for your time, and I look forward to hearing from you.

Best,

(Your Signature Here)
Jonathan Internstein

Hint: If you don't know the name of the person you are addressing, begin the letter with "To Whom It May Concern." And at the end of the letter, your last words should be either "Sincerely," "Best," or "Regards," and then sign your name in black or blue ink, typing out your full name below it.

FROM THE INTERN FILES OF THE INTERNSHIP COORDINATOR

We do year-round recruiting to over 350 universities to fulfill the needs of our program. We also post on our Web site when we are looking for interns. After reviewing the résumés (résumés with spelling errors, or cover letters that call us by the wrong name, are immediately rejected, for obvious reasons), I set up interviews. Rejection letters are sent to those who didn't make the cut. Sometimes an applicant lives far away, so we'll have a phone interview. After interviewing the candidate, we make a decision, and then I notify the candidate.

FIND YOUR SCHOOL'S INTERNSHIP DIRECTOR | CHAPTER 3

 EVERYONE KNOWS THAT COLLEGES AND THEIR PROGRAMS ARE RUN BY A CONGLOMERATE OF DEANS, DEPARTMENT HEADS, CHAIRS, AND PEOPLE with other dubious titles. Internship programs are no different. The first step in the process of becoming an intern is to seek out your school's internship director and set up a one-on-one meeting with him or her to talk about what field you may be interested in, and what opportunities there are in those fields around your school.

You'll need to ask how the credit system works at your school, what kind of requirements are necessary to receive those credits—outside of simply showing up—and when you can begin. It varies from school to school, but most universities require you to be in a specific year before interning, and allow a certain number of credits to be earned.

FROM THE INTERN FILES OF THE INTERNSHIP DIRECTOR

Students should ask themselves the following questions:

What are my reasons for wanting to intern?
What are my interests?
What are my work values?
What are my skills?
What are my career dreams?
What do I want to try to accomplish?

But the most important thing a person can do to begin the internship process is walk into the internship office with a résumé. It's so critical that a student has a résumé and knows how to present himself or herself on paper—all part of the early stages of landing an internship.

When you meet with your school's internship department, make sure you have a résumé in your hand. It doesn't have to be perfect—in fact, one of the questions you should ask the internship office is, "How does my résumé look, and can I improve it?" You should also bring a notebook and a pen so you can jot down key information—and get used to looking the part.

Ask about what kind of resources the school provides in order to help students look for internships, and what outside resources they recommend. Internship directors have a passion for helping students navigate their futures throughout the college experience.

It is of the utmost importance that you forge—and maintain—a strong and honest relationship with your internship director and advisor while you are in the internship program. You need an ally. When situations begin to arise (and they likely will) that you can't handle alone, you need to have an advocate at all times, both in the office and at your school. Having a good relationship with your internship director or advisor means you will always have someone to turn to.

The goal of an internship program is not only to have students begin carving out their own careers, but to have companies call and say, "We want more interns just like Johnny." This makes the program successful, makes you look great, and possibly begins a new relationship between a company and an academic institution, which could help you get a job down the road.

"THERE'S NO SUCH THING AS AN EXCEPTION" —GARY

I went to school in Washington, D.C., and had a friend who interned for this political think tank that he said would be exactly what I was looking for. Anyhow, I met his boss and he had a look at my thin résumé, and after a brief meeting, said he'd be happy to have me as an intern the following semester. I thought, *Great! Now all I have to do is figure out how that works with school scheduling and stuff—simple.*

Not so much. What I found was that since I didn't really get any information from my school's internship office—an office that was very well known and easy to find—I had made a grave mistake. See, it was already November and the fall semester was winding down. And I had practically promised my friend's boss that I would intern for him during the following semester.

When I went to the internship office and tried to meet with someone, they told me to come back the following Monday to meet the internship director to talk about what I wanted to do and when I wanted to do it. I thanked the guy at the desk and went home.

Come Monday, I showed up at the internship office with nothing—no résumé, no class schedule—nothing. The woman who ran the program called me into her office and said, "So, what year are you?" I answered, "Sophomore."

She replied, "Oh, so you've already registered for next semester, I take it?" Then it all clicked. I had indeed registered for next semester. How could I intern, too?

She told me that I needed to come in around September to

begin advisement and register one of my classes as "Internship Seminar" so that I would have time to go to my internship, and I would receive credit.

I pleaded with her: "But you don't understand, I already told my friend's boss that I would intern at his think tank, and I can't back out now! Can't you, like, write me a note, or make an exception or something?"

Her reply was simple, all-encompassing, and final: "There *are* no exceptions when it comes to business."

And in the end, I interned the next summer for that company, although my lack of preparation definitely rubbed a few people the wrong way. Once you enter the work world, particularly as an intern, a deadline is a deadline, and that's the end of it.

BAD NEWS FIRST: MOST PEOPLE RARELY, IF EVER, GET EXACTLY THE INTERNSHIP THEY DESPERATELY WANT. SOME PEOPLE WANT *REAL TIME WITH BILL MAHER*, but they end up with *The McEnroe Show*. Others want to intern for Larry King but end up on a press tour with Don King. It happens.

The good news is there are tons of resources available to help you find something that fits with your goals.

First, explore your connections. Who do you know, how do you know them, and have you slept with their children who are your age? Key questions. Let's say you want to work in the record industry, and that your top three choices are Def Jam Recordings, Bad Boy Entertainment, and J Records. First, rack your brain, your black books, your cell phone numbers, your e-mail contacts, your friends, and your family to see if you have a connection to anyone at these companies. Even if you don't know anyone personally, maybe there are two degrees of separation between you and a low-level staff member at one of the three companies. The truth is that most people get jobs through these more distant connections, rather than through close ones.

So say you find a friend of a friend of a friend at J Records. Your first step should be to set up a casual meeting to introduce yourself and begin the process of gluing your lips to their ass until you've gotten what you want out of them. That might sound like a joke, and it sort of is, but it is also the harsh reality of what it takes to get what you want in your career. If you're lucky, you'll actually get along with and maybe even genuinely like them. But more important, they need to like you.

Forget your opinions and your perception of your contact as a person, and sell yourself like a piece of high-priced meat. Get yourself sold and eaten alive as quickly as possible. This (the meeting to get the job) is going to be something you probably don't have much experience with, which will show. That's perfectly fine. The key to wooing your new connection is to appear optimistic about your future, yet cautious about the fact that it's really just begun. You want to find a way to make up for your lack of experience, usually with a noticeable sense of confidence. Confidence is intangible and cannot be easily faked. So don't try to sound egotistical and arrogant, but rather, optimistic, fresh but not naive, strong, and composed. Just be yourself.

The bottom line is that this person is going to be sticking his or her neck out for you, which means that he or she is going to be represented by you to some degree. Recommending someone, particularly an intern, is an enormous favor and one that comes with great responsibility and gratitude on the part of the recommendee. In other words, don't get in over your head or lie to get the gig. Once you do get an internship, you're on the observation deck, and the person who gave you a reference will be too—so don't take it lightly.

But again: Just be yourself. More than likely, your connection will be someone who isn't much older than you, and who has probably had similar struggles. So don't try to be anything but you, because perceptive people—particularly people who are around your age—will see right through anything on your end that is contrived. Tell the person the same things you told your school's internship director: Why you want the internship, what qualifies you for the internship, what you can bring to an organization, and what you want to get out of it. As always, be honest. If you present yourself wholeheartedly and with integrity, and a company—or in this case, a single person—doesn't think you'd be a good fit, then you probably weren't meant to work there in the first place. That's perfectly fine. If you lie about what you want, where you want to be, and what you think you can do in order to get an internship, not only will you likely fail, but you'll probably be unhappy, and that's the worst-case scenario. This is an internship, not a job; you don't get paid and you don't have many bills to pay, so you still have room to get some career clarification, trying things out as you go, not simply doing what needs to be done just to make rent on time. Why waste time when you've still got it?

"DADDY'S LITTLE BOYS AND GIRLS" —KARL

People think connections are everything—well, they're not too far off. I was given a summer internship after my freshman year in college by my uncle, who ran a top New York City law firm. A week or so before the internship was to begin, he called me to tell me that there was a mandatory drug test for all new employees, which included interns. Okay, that was very bad news. I was no druggie, but I smoked my fair share of pot and *definitely* would have gotten caught.

But I didn't panic. I figured I'd do everything in my power to flush my system in the next few days, and if I still failed the test, my uncle would get me out of it. So I went to my local pharmacy and explained the situation to the guy behind the counter. He gave me a few alleged remedies to totally flush out my system. "You'll be clean as a whistle," he exclaimed.

So I put the bong away and drank my cleansing formulas noon and night. The day of the test came, and I didn't even feel the least bit nervous. So I went in, took the test, then headed back to my house and went directly for the weed. I smoked all night long.

The following Monday I got a call from my uncle. He said that he wanted me to come in and speak to him right away. Now, my uncle was a cool guy, but he wasn't about to throw his career away over his imbecilic nephew. When I arrived, he said that my drug test basically concluded that I had been attempting to flush my system. I was caught red-handed.

He said I had no choice but to go to the testing center and take a new test immediately. Anyway, I took the test again and failed it—obviously. And when the phone rang, my uncle was singing a very different tune than I had expected.

"What the hell is wrong with you?" he yelled.

"Uncle Steve, I'm sorry. You'll still get me this internship, right?" I begged.

"Are you out of your mind? I have to worry about my own job because of you! Why the hell would I plead your case?"

And that was it. He hung up the phone and I was without an internship, still owing my school's internship director an explanation about why I had my internship terminated, and left with the unenviable task of finding a new gig right away. But what ended up happening with me that summer is really superfluous. The point is that even though I was basically a family hire, one of daddy's little boys and girls, as it were, failing a drug test—or any unacceptable behavior, for that matter—is more important to a company than a family tie.

Most companies won't give you extra-special treatment while you screw around thinking you can just get away with it. I never even got the chance to deal with the social etiquette of an office, because I never made it past the first step. Had they hired me anyway and real employees found out about the situation, rest assured, everyone would have been up in arms. In retrospect, I'm glad I didn't slip through the cracks. But if you do want to make it, potheads beware!

Once you've tried all of your connections, check out your school's database (ask about it in the school's career counseling office if you're not sure where to look). In the database you will find listings, by industry and location, of internship opportunities and contact information for the appropriate person at each site. At this stage, having a strong relationship with your internship advisors and director is very important. While there are many roads to travel in terms of finding available internships, none will be less windy than the road that runs directly through your school. The people in the internship and career offices likely have standing relationships with particular companies, and if not, they will be able to give you background information on any company they're familiar with. The bottom line is that your school is one of the best connections you have.

For example, some New York City universities have a great relationship with MTV. If a student wants an internship at MTV, the internship director can easily make a phone call and help the student get the internship. But if the people at MTV receive a résumé without the recommendation of the internship director, the student is far less likely to get the internship than if they had had a letter of reference to accompany their résumé. You might have connections all around you, and if you don't use them, you'll lack credibility and run the risk of appearing somehow suspect.

However, one of the great things about interning is learning to act on your own, because then you are the only person responsible for your actions (or lack thereof). In other words, you'll know that you didn't get a call back from Microsoft because *you* forgot to send them your résumé.

Your school may not have a relationship with a company that

you're interested in, and you may have no connection whatsoever. In this case, you'll have to do it on your own, with whatever help and advice you can get from your school. But you've got to be proactive. Find contact information from the company's Web site or from the Yellow Pages—dial 411 if you have to. If you're checking a company's Web site, you'll want to look for icons that say "jobs," "career," or "employment." Then you'll find the name of the person you should contact for internships.

Some prefer calling; others prefer to roll with the twenty-first century and do everything online. However, it's tough to get a résumé looked at by blindly sending it to Human Resources. Companies might not have a specific set of instructions for internships, and if they do, they probably receive hundreds of résumés a month and only ever get to a few—those that come with references, or those that are sent directly from a school staff member to Human Resources, or that are sent to an employee who can in turn recommend you to the appropriate person. Try to find the name of a person who will actually open the envelope and read what's inside.

This is the technology era, so make the most of it. Go to Google and search for internships and companies that interest you. Go to Yahoo! and search their job listings and see if you can find internships listed among "real" jobs. For cities and towns that have it, go to Craigslist and search "internships." Check trade papers. Talk to people while you're socializing and begin networking, letting everyone you meet know where you want to work. Once you begin the hunt, you have to represent yourself and look for opportunities at all times, whether you're at the library or at the club.

Unless a company specifically says "no phone calls" on their Web site, it's always best to speak with a live person before sending anything off. It's simple: Call an organization's general phone number and say, "Hi, my name is Joe Smith. I'm a student at the University of Michigan, and I'd like some information about applying for an internship, please." Then you'll probably be given the name of the internship coordinator or someone in Human Resources, and if you're lucky, a phone number to boot. Here's where initiative comes in. More often than not, depending on the size of a company, you'll be told to simply send a résumé and cover letter to the main office "and someone will get back to you." Only as a last resort should you send a résumé to the main office to languish in a pile. At the very least, you should try to get a specific desk, the Human Resources department, or preferably the name of the person to whom you should send the package. If you just send it to the mailroom, it might not ever make it to the right desk.

What if the operator says that he or she can't give you any more information? First, be persistent. Call back and see if you get someone else who may be a bit more helpful. Then, with grace and maturity, start to . . . well . . . beg, saying something like, "I don't mean to trouble you, but I can't seem to get my résumé to the right place, and I'd *really* appreciate a little help." Hopefully this will get you a name—if not, just send it to the company's Human Resources department, to the attention of the internship coordinator.

Pay close attention to the way you send off your application. Of course, the package should contain a cover letter, a résumé, and any supplementary material the company requires (such as a writing sample). The contents of the package should be attached by paper clip, not staples, tape, or Krazy Glue. And pay attention to the order of the material as well. The first page should be your cover letter, followed by your résumé, and then internship-specific contents. Make sure the package has a return address on it, and that your résumé has your contact information. Send the package in a nicely sealed envelope with the address in neat, legible handwriting. The package must be neat and aesthetically pleasing—don't write the address in graffiti or with bright red ink for effect.

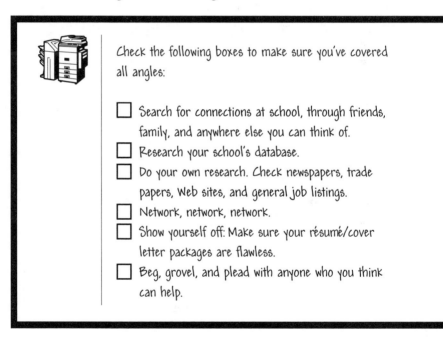

Check the following boxes to make sure you've covered all angles:

☐ Search for connections at school, through friends, family, and anywhere else you can think of.

☐ Research your school's database.

☐ Do your own research. Check newspapers, trade papers, Web sites, and general job listings.

☐ Network, network, network.

☐ Show yourself off: Make sure your résumé/cover letter packages are flawless.

☐ Beg, grovel, and plead with anyone who you think can help.

THE INTERVIEW
(WITH ALEXIS FELDMAN)

CHAPTER 5

 AH, THE INTERNSHIP INTERVIEW: A FIVE- TO FIFTEEN-MINUTE PERIOD DURING WHICH YOU TRY TO WOO THE INTERVIEWER WITH YOUR SKILLS, your competence, your ability to lie through your teeth, and your smile. Yes, smile. The most important thing to remember during an interview is to show those pearly whites. You need to exude a positive attitude through the tone of your voice and that big, shining smile on your face. Interviews are all about selling yourself and, however secretly, sucking up. Giving off the right attitude during the brief time with your interviewer is crucial.

There are other superficial components to an interview, like a nice, firm handshake. Some people judge a person's character by their handshake. Get that down before you start the interviewing process by practicing with people you know. Along with that solid grip, master the art of eye contact. People say, "When you don't make eye contact with someone, it's like slapping them in the face." That may be a bit extreme, but poor eye contact makes you look scared at a time when it's imperative that you appear confident. These are easy things to prepare for, so practice. Get a mirror and a friend. You want to interview from a vantage point of confidence, and experienced or not, the more you practice the more it will show.

Interviews can make or break you, so research the company and the industry the company is in, and before you go, take a few minutes to talk to yourself. It sounds weird, but you gotta do it. Make a list of questions the interviewer might ask and then come up with interesting answers. Think of tangible examples to spice up your responses, and anecdotes that show that you're smart and accomplished. Try to make sure the interviewer knows you're a hard worker and a fast learner. Always keep in mind that you are selling yourself. You want to sound confident, intelligent, and experienced.

An interview will always be more difficult if you don't prepare, practice, and try to perfect your answers. You can easily be caught off guard by something the interviewer asks and then sound like a bumbling idiot trying to come up with an answer. There's the story of a major New York financial group that asks their interviewees, about midway through the interview, without warning, if they know the number of gas stations in Manhattan. What's the point? Simply to see the manner in which the subject handles being thrown a curveball after fifty straight fastballs. You need to be prepared for anything. Otherwise, you might look like a fool. Not a good look for you at all.

FROM THE INTERN FILES OF THE INTERNSHIP COORDINATOR

In addition to a solid résumé and cover letter, someone with a great, outgoing personality and a positive attitude really goes far. An intern is considered lower than an entry-level position; an intern serves as an assistant to the staff, often doing all the things that employees don't want to do, so a positive attitude plays a huge role.

Think of preparing for an interview like preparing for a presentation in school. Before you stand before a classroom full of people, you rehearse what you want to say and how you want to say it, knowing full well that you'll likely be probed in unexpected ways. That's exactly what you do for an interview. Stand in front of the mirror or walk around your room preparing answers to potential questions. Whatever works, just talk out what you want to say.

You are competing for an internship against God knows how many other applicants, so make the best out of the little time you have to show who you are. You're selling yourself, but you should sell who you actually are, not who you wish you could be. Just like when you're making a contact or meeting a potential reference, present the best of you, not an idealized version of the person you strive to be. So once again, just be yourself.

While utilizing your time to talk yourself up, talk your interviewer up as well. Complimenting him or her and the company couldn't hurt, could it? You don't want to be a brownnoser, but who doesn't appreciate a little compliment here and there? You want to come across as polite and friendly, so don't sit there and spew out compliment after compliment. If you do, you'll probably be shown the door real fast. The compliments should be about the company, the nature of the company's business, or something of that sort. Don't talk about the interviewer's fabulous shoes! Tell him or her the truth about why you're interested in working there. Is the company a market leader? Do they make a great product? Have you heard everyone who works there is nice? Tell them that!

Good compliment: "I can already tell, from the employees I met on the way in, that your office has a great vibe and good people."

Bad compliment: "I really like that tie, sir. I have one just like it myself."

Enough of the introductory stuff. The bulk of the interview is the question-and-answer period. There are several staple questions that most interviewers will ask, no matter what area of work the internship is in. Here are some generic yet frequently asked interview questions. Read them and answer them out loud, paying particular attention to the wording in your reply. Practice, practice, practice!

Generic Interview Question #1: "Why do you want this internship?"

Perfect Response Example #1: "Even though this will be my first internship, I have such a love for music that I feel I'll be able to learn anything you want me to very quickly. I'm not only a fast learner, but I'm very dedicated to your artists and your company's mission."

Imperfect Response #1: "Because I want a good résumé for when I look for a real job."

Generic Interview Question #2: "What will *you* bring to this internship that others won't?"

Perfect Response Example #2: "Well, I'm a lifelong musician, but I'm a business major in college. Even though I may not have the experience, I know what artists need, what people want to hear, and I am learning the business aspect every day in class. So, by combining my artistic talents with my pragmatic side, I can bring something special to your company."

Imperfect Response #2: "I feel like I'm really a good fit for this position."

Generic Interview Question #3: "What past experience do you think will help you at this internship?"

Perfect Response Example #3: "I'm good at working closely with people as well as independently. I always make deadlines and am very familiar, through my coursework and personal interests, with what you do here."

Imperfect Response #3: "I'd have to say it would be working at Dairy Queen. You know, because it was so, like, intense and high-stress."

Use these answers as a template for your own perfect answers. And try not to sound like a robot. It's a challenge, but by personalizing these answers and speaking clearly, with diction that's intelligent and professional, you'll blow away your interviewer.

As the interview winds down, the person interviewing you will likely ask, "Do you have any questions for me?" You'd better! Answering questions intelligently is half the battle. The other half is asking questions. This is why researching the company and its field is important. You want to be knowledgeable and appear interested. This is a golden opportunity for you to subtly sell yourself and address any real questions you may have. These questions should be specific, well constructed, and applicable to interns only! Here are some examples of good questions, as well as some you may want to stay away from.

Good Question: "Since I will be interning for the A&R department, can you describe what I would be working on or what my day-to-day responsibilities would be?"

Bad Question: "Are there a lot of good restaurants in this neighborhood?"

Good Question: "What does it take for an intern to set him- or herself apart from other interns at your company?"

Bad Question: "If I do well, will you pay me?"

Good Question: "How much would you say you rely on your interns on a daily basis?"

Bad Question: "Will I have mad work to do?"

Remember, ask questions that you really want to know the answer to, as well as questions that show your interest and allow you to appear well informed and inquisitive at the same time.

"PRACTICE MAKES PERFECT" —PETER

Before my interview for an internship at a major hip-hop and urban culture magazine, I asked myself the question, "So, why do you want this internship?" over, and over, and over, and over again. It took me two days to perfect my answer, and I knew it was great because it was true. Not only had I figured out why I wanted to be there, but I sounded articulate and ambitious. But it wasn't that easy. I had rehearsed so many times that what I was saying had lost its meaning. I became so caught up with my delivery that I somehow forgot what the opportunity really meant to me.

Here's how it went down:

Interviewer sits down, says, "So tell me why you want to intern here."

My plan was to say, "Working here would perfectly combine my three favorite things in the world: Music, particularly hip-hop; writing, particularly journalism; and youth culture, particularly in an urban setting." Doesn't that sound great?

With sweat pouring from my brow, I replied, "Well, music, I love music . . . no, I mean hip-hop is the . . . actually, I'd combine my musical love for my writing love if I were here. You know, love to write, love to listen to music! That's what it's all about!"

Realizing how royally I'd screwed this up, I tried to start over.

"Well, I want to combine my three favorite passions," I said emphatically. "Music, writing, and . . . and . . . and . . ." Yep—couldn't remember what the third one was.

Sensing my nervousness, the interviewer sort of slowed me down and asked a few other questions. I was on the verge of passing out. By the time I had slowed down, I did make the point that interning in music journalism, particularly for a publication that dealt primarily with a genre of music that I loved and respected, was absolutely perfect for me. And I did, in the end, land the internship.

I wouldn't advise anyone not to practice for their interview, but I'd be sure to monitor yourself in terms of how much is too much. Even though you have to talk to the mirror, random people on the street, and your pets to practice the right amount, eventually someone oughta tell you to stick a sock in it. If they don't, tell yourself. After a while, if you try too hard, what you're saying loses its meaning and sounds contrived.

In retrospect, I think if I had focused more on my feelings than on the exact words while practicing, it would have been easier for me to remember what I really wanted to say. After all, it's easier to remember a few key words than a whole script.

While you're at your interview, do a bit of a sociological study of the office.

- Pay close attention to what people are wearing so that if you get the job, you'll know the dress code.
- Try to get a feel for who's who.
- Notice the volume in the office. Are people listening to

music at their desks, or is it dead silent?
- Do employees appear to be chatting each other up while they do their work, or is it one of those quiet offices in which the silence is actually distracting?
- Are there any potential hookups on your floor?
- Do they appear interested in a potential intern?
- Remember, you're only there for an hour or less, so make sure to stick to the important stuff.

Once the interview ends—and after you give a nice departing handshake—there is still one last thing you need to do. You want the interviewer to remember you, so a great way to keep yourself in his/her mind is the follow-up letter.

Dear Mr. Z:

It was a pleasure meeting with you today to discuss interning for the A&R department. Thank you for taking the time to see me. I look forward to hearing from you.

Best,

Johnny Internstein

Include something specific from your meeting, but try to keep it simple, short, and to the point. Your interviewer will appreciate the note. It's a nice gesture, but it's also absolutely essential. It makes you stand out and speaks highly of your character. It confirms that you really want the job, which certainly can't hurt. If you've been corresponding by e-mail, feel free to send it that way. Otherwise, type and send a formal letter with your signature penned neatly at the bottom. The follow-up letter is crucial, so give it close attention.

| CHAPTER 6

 THERE ARE OCCASIONS WHEN YOU WILL FIND YOURSELF IN THE UNENVIABLE, THOUGH FAIRLY COMMON, SITUATION OF HAVING APPLIED FOR AN internship but not getting hired. Worse yet, you might not have applied anywhere else.

There's no rule that says, "You must apply for six internships per semester." You have to decide how many applications to send out yourself. If you have a close connection at an internship you are applying for, then you'll need only one or two fallback choices. In general, a good policy is probably to apply to at least three internships. Hopefully, your school's internship program will be able to help troubleshoot. If you really can't seem to land anything, they might even be able to find you one or switch you out of the program for that semester. It's not the end of the world.

On the other end of the spectrum, you might get more than one offer. The most important thing is to be professional and respectful even to those internship opportunities you decline. If you get one offer but you're waiting on other responses, just say that you'll get back to them with a decision as soon as possible (but ask them when they need your answer, and make sure you tell them by the date they give you). As for the offers that you don't want, write a grateful, professional letter explaining that you're respectfully declining their offer.

Dear Mr. Z:

Thank you for offering me the opportunity to intern for your company this semester. Unfortunately, I have decided to accept another offer.

Sincerely,

Johnny Internstein

You don't have to explain anything in detail—in fact, it's best you don't. Just thank the employer, and keep that door wide open for the future. Who knows, after working for Mr. Z's competitor, you may go crawling back to Mr. Z himself. Remember: short, simple, and grateful.

All right—you just got yourself an internship. Time to figure out what to do when you get there.

Tip: **School comes first.** Before you start your internship, be sure to work out your schedule way in advance. Work around your class schedule. Most companies will tell you how many hours they require of you per week; just make sure you can do it before you commit to anything. This is another time you can use your school's internship office.
Otherwise, you could find yourself helpless in these situations, leading to a scheduling conflict that can't be amended. This could potentially ruin your career and result in homelessness. Not really, but you certainly won't be doing yourself any favors.

PART II | THE FIRST DAY

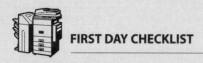 **FIRST DAY CHECKLIST**

The Night Before Your First Day
- Get painfully wasted.
- Stay up all night worrying about your first day.
- Don't do your laundry—worry about what to wear in the morning.

The Morning Of
- Call in late in the morning, then show up around noon saying you barely made it.
- Smoke a cigarette as you walk through the door and stomp it in your boss's office.
- Set your cell phone's ring to oppressively loud rap music.

If you'd rather not get fired on your first day, try this:

The Night Before
- Get your outfit ready.
- Have a mellow night; get to bed early.
- Shower, or make sure your roommates won't be in the way when you're getting ready in the morning.
- Plan your route to get to the office.

The Morning Of
- Nourish yourself: OJ, eggs, coffee, or your own favorite breakfast.
- Be twenty minutes early, but don't walk in until five minutes before you're supposed to be there.
- Turn your cell phone off.
- Be positive and remain calm.

IT SOUNDS CRAZY, BUT, BELIEVE IT OR NOT, LOTS OF PEOPLE IN THIS COUNTRY JUDGE YOU SOLELY BY YOUR APPEARANCE. NO, SERIOUSLY, CAN YOU BELIEVE that? And nothing is more influential than a first impression. You should have been paying close attention to other people's getups while you were in the office for an interview, but that plan's not flawless. Maybe your internship is in a different city, or perhaps you had a phone interview. Maybe you interviewed during the summer, and now it's fall and the dress code changes with the season. How are you supposed to know what to wear?

ASK! There is absolutely nothing wrong with calling a few days before you're scheduled to start your internship and asking your new boss to give you the details of the company's policy on appearance. However, as always, you have to sound professional.

Say something like: "Good afternoon, Mr. Moldoun, this is Johnny Internstein. How are you? I'm excited to start next week."[3]

"Hi, John, I'm fine."

---

3. Now pause and let him answer you! If you ask someone how they are, don't forget to pause.

"Well, I'm calling because I wanted to ask about the dress code. Is it formal or business casual?"

Tip: Always call your supervisor Mr. or Ms. at first. Wait until they ask you to call them by their first name before you do it. It might also be a good idea to avoid calling anyone "sir" or "ma'am," because it makes people feel old. If you're working for the military or the president, disregard that last bit.

Hopefully your supervisor will remember that he hired you and give you an answer. The key is to ask how interns—not real employees—are expected to dress. Since you probably spend most of your time in jeans and T-shirts, being the young, ultra-cool cat that you are, you may have a little shopping to do. You want to fit in, after all. Dress well; look like you're ready for a "real" job, but don't come so underdressed or overdressed that you stick out. Even though what you wear is important, let your game do the talking. It's sort of like you're Clark Kent, waiting to unleash Superman on important things like faxing and filing decade-old paperwork! YEAH!

If you can't find out what the dress code is at your workplace, business casual is a great place to start, since it's the most common dress code for interns. Basically, business casual is code for "look as boring and plain as is humanly possible."

For the guys, we're talking khakis, very simple dress shoes—nothing too flashy, of course—and a neatly pressed button-down oxford shirt. The belt should be subdued; the ice your Uncle Ray bought you for Christmas needs to be tucked into your shirt. Got that? Ice *inside* the shirt. Good.

For women, business casual is just as boring as it is for men. A pair of nice pants or a knee-length skirt, an unrevealing button-down shirt or a sweater, simple jewelry, and yep, some plain dress shoes.

It may sound depressing, but just go ahead and buy some simple clothing—the basics. Business casual is a loose term; you'll probably want to look like part of the team. After you've been there for a few days or a week, you might want to go out and buy more if you're standing out too far from the crowd.

 Rule of thumb for business casual: Black pants and a blue shirt work at all times for both men and women at any office.

There are many offices in which the executives will be in full suits, but their low-level employees are wearing business casual. This is a very typical corporate "up yours." People may say that it's a very easy way to tell who's who in the office, but really, it's just a nice way for more powerful people to feel, well, more powerful. So don't try to rock the boat; just dress as you are asked to dress and don't worry too much about it.

Tip: Business casual = dull, simple, plain, inoffensive, does not cause unnecessary attention.

What if your supervisor tells you to wear anything you want? This is a tricky one, because you have to mesh your own personal style with the look of the rest of the office. For example, if you're working for a hyper-trendy company, you can just wear whatever you would normally wear. If you try to change your style to look more like others in the office, you will appear just as contrived as your outfit. If you're not particularly into fashion or trends in the first place, but you find yourself at a company that is, it's really still best to just be yourself, even if you think it won't be impressive. Be comfortable in your intern skin, no matter who makes your jeans.

For those on the other side of the fashion scale, it's always important not to be too cool for school. Not even in style-conscious, fashion-heavy kinds of offices. If you're the best-dressed employee there, and you're not even really an employee, rest assured someone will be jealous, and that will turn to resentment, and resentment is one of the most powerful forces in office politics. If the wrong person resents you because they assume that you're a super-rich college kid with no bills to pay, or if they think that you think you're cooler than everyone else, they are in a position to do what they will with you, and that could mean you'll get fired. So be yourself, but tone it down a bit if you think your fabulousness offends or intimidates employees. And if you find yourself at an office where the better you dress, the more you're respected, then don't show up wearing the same thing every day.

Dealing with office politics is a very sticky thing—even when it comes to something as simple as how you dress. Remember that these rules are not set in stone by any means. The key to dressing appropriately is to stay informed, and the way to stay informed is to ask when you're unsure.

If you have a summer internship, you may have different hours on Fridays, and perhaps a slightly altered dress code, known in the corporate world as "casual Fridays." This is an important thing to ask about. If you work on Fridays, find out if there are summer hours, and follow that up by asking whether the dress code on Fridays is different from the rest of the week.

There are some offices that will require full business attire, from the suit to the suspenders. This can be problematic. You might not own a suit, or maybe you only have one, leaving you with a gigantic dry-cleaning bill or with the nickname "that smelly intern." If you own one suit, just keep your shower running all day while your suit hangs from the bathroom doorknob—then you'll look like Chris Farley in David Spade's coat soaked in water; it'll be awesome!

But seriously, if you're not in a position to go out and buy a few suits, the best thing to do, after begging your parents, selling dope, acting homeless to collect change on the streets, and engaging in prostitution, is to simply sit down with your supervisor, or someone you feel comfortable with, and address the situation.

Politely explain that while you understand that as an intern you are required to dress a certain way, you simply don't have the money, but you want to look your best as a representative of the company. Most likely you'll be told not to worry about it, but believe it or not, sometimes companies have valued an intern so much that they actually paid for new suits so that the intern would stick around a while. As long as you're always up-front, honest, and professional, the possibilities are endless.

Tip: If you don't have what you need, there are always relatively inexpensive department stores like Loehmann's, Old Navy, Target, and Kmart (hey, there's nothing wrong with the mega-mart!). It's worth spending some money to have the right kind of clothes.

Always ask as many questions as you need in order to look the part. Dressing appropriately means you're taking a step toward fitting in, and that's vital in the business world. It will eventually become routine. It's not that complicated, and you'll get used to it. You'd better—you'll be working till you're sixty-five!

"THE SUIT" —VINCENT

I was nineteen, barely a sophomore, and had never interned before. I landed my dream internship at a major, but indie-feeling, film company in Los Angeles, where I went to college. I had an interview, but we met on campus at a school internship fair, so it was very informal.

During the winter I called my contact at the company several times to solidify the hours and days I'd be working, and we discussed my transportation costs—I even got a small stipend. But I had one burning question I never got around to asking because I thought I'd sound like an idiot. The question was simple: What are interns supposed to wear?

My birthday fell over winter break, and with my new, high-powered internship in mind, I decided I'd ask my parents for a new suit so that I'd fit in right away. I figured it was better to be over-dressed than underdressed, even at a small company.

The suit was gray with a faint pinstripe—professional, but chic. *I'll blow them all away,* I thought. *I'll look like I belong.* So on the first day of my internship, I got up around seven thirty and threw on my suit, new shoes, and expensive cotton socks. I was armed and ready to take on the film world. As I entered the office, I noticed that not another soul, including the guy who introduced himself as "the guy you'll answer to if you really screw up," had anything but jeans and T-shirts on. Naturally there were slight variations, particularly for the women, but on the whole, I was in black tie, and the rest of the company's twenty or so employees were dressed for a night at the Waffle House.

After I made it through the windy, seemingly endless halls of the office—mellow tunes softly creeping out from beneath the cubicles—I reached the desk of my internship coordinator.

I tapped her on the shoulder and said, "Hi, I'm here to start my internship."

"What? What's your name?" she said, looking utterly perplexed.

"Don't you remember me? I'm Jim—starting an internship today."

"Jim? *Jim!* Jesus Christ! What are you wearing that suit for?" she belted out.

"I—I—I just thought that's what all offices required," I said nervously. Mind you, there were about eight people standing nearby, all watching this fiasco. "I'm so sorry. I just wanted to impress you guys."

"Impress us?" she replied. "If you want to impress us, it'll be through your work, your effort, and your drive—not your flashy suit."

I took a deep breath and said, "Okay, I understand. I was just trying to look the part and—"

"Look the part!" she interrupted me abruptly. "You're an intern. Your parents pay your bills and you still have homework. What *part*, exactly, are you referring to?"

"Okay," I said. "I completely get it. But what about today?"

"Well, you can start by asking me what *is* appropriate dress code for an intern, like you should have done in the first place, and then you can take off the jacket and tie and untuck that shirt. Then you can make us all coffee."

I wore the remnants of that suit all day, and here I am two years later working at the same company in twenty-dollar jeans and a hooded sweatshirt. My first day stank, to say the least, but it also made me a part of the company and gave everyone a good laugh, even if it was at my expense.

***DING!* THE ALARM RINGS. YOU ROLL OVER, FIGHT-
ING EVERY LAST BRAIN CELL, MUSCLE, AND
INSTINCT THAT'S SAYING, *COME ON, MAN, DON'T*
go to work. Eventually you make a full turn over toward the alarm and
wham! You smack that thing with every morsel of strength you have
in you.

Once the beeping-dinging-ringing of your trusty alarm comes to a
halt, you find yourself at a crossroads . . . a serious crossroads. You could
just go back to sleep, basking in the glory of air conditioning and the
fruits of the fridge. But no! Not you! Not today! You want the truth
about the work world and goddamn it, you *can* handle it! Who needs
sleep, anyway? It's your time to shine.

You let out a final yawn, wipe that grime out of the corners of your beet-
red eyes, and *bam!* Your foot has hit the floor. It's all downhill from here.
There will be no greater task than forcing the bottom of your right foot to
hit your filthy floor at eight o'clock in the morning. If you can do that, you
can do anything an intern has ever been asked to do and then some!

You go to the bathroom and get directly into the shower. While you're in the shower, you start to calm your mind. You think of anything, absolutely anything, besides the fact that you're about to go perch yourself on the observation deck having no idea what to expect. As your body completely cleanses itself of summer school, regular morning classes, and the stagnancy of a college classroom, you start to feel damn special. You're an intern now—you're free—get a move on!

So now you're clean, your hair looks right, your coffee is calling your name from up the block, and all you need to do is get dressed. But you're a step ahead; you already know what to wear. You go to your room, throw on the outfit you prepped the night before, and you're off!

You leave your house and go directly to the source of all good first days: Starbucks! Or better yet, an independent coffeehouse with a superior blend. You take that first sip and move on to get some eggs in your system—a good, if slightly rushed, breakfast is essential. You hop into your car, cab, train, or bus and begin your journey—coffee and bacon, egg, and cheese sandwich[4] in hand—to the first day of your new life.

Tip: If you're driving, don't speed; the last thing you need is to show up an hour late on your first day and have to explain that you got pulled over for doing eighty in a thirty zone because you didn't want to be late. The response you will inevitably get is that you should have left earlier, and you'll have no retort.

---

4. Or toast and grapes. Whatever.

Finally! You arrive at your office. The sweat begins to trickle uncontrollably down your back, and you wonder if it's soaked through your shirt. You ask yourself, *Am I really ready for this? Can I really do this?* But, you remind yourself, these tensions are normal. You can do it, and you will do it! Get your ass in that front door and you'll have made a giant leap toward success, fame, fortune, and a corner office.

You approach the office and are greeted by a receptionist. You keep your head up and your smile showing. You're confident, not arrogant or cocky. Okay, maybe you're insecure and scared, but you remain calm and humble on the outside. You say, "Hi, I'm John, and I'm starting my internship for Mr. Moldoun in Ad Sales today."

With a smile, the receptionist says, "Just one moment, I'll let him know you're here." The tension and sweat resurface. *Remain calm!* The receptionist says you can head back now. No time to think, just move, man, move! You step through the doors into the endless world of matching gray cubicles and walk through the room with a series of quiet greetings. Keep smiling! Are you smiling? You're not smiling wide enough! This is serious!

You reach your supervisor and *bam!* Out comes the hand. Are you ready for your first firm handshake? *Of course you're ready!* You take that sweaty palm out of your pocket, do a quick de-sweat maneuver, and confidently shake your supervisor's hand. You're prepared for anything: filing, faxing, copying. No, not copying! But wait, Mr. Moldoun says, "Hey, John. We're so glad you're here. Can you fill out an SJ2G4 and bring it to Rob in the supplies room so Dave can get some new file-folder holders for project #A678890044Q?"

What's the problem? You don't understand what was just asked of you? That is *not* a problem. It's the perfect time to ask your first question! It's going to happen sooner or later, so you may as well break the ice.

After you order the supplies, Mr. Moldoun tells you to just hang out for a while. You do everything possible to look busy to avoid sitting there staring awkwardly at the guy in the cubicle across from you who's playing solitaire and mumbling profanities at his reflection every time he draws a bad card.

You decide to walk around the office and start introducing yourself to people and acclimate yourself with your surroundings as much as possible. You take the long way to the bathroom and take mental notes of who sits where and how to get to the coffee, fax, and copy machines as quickly as possible. You're keeping your eyes open for any friendships you may see hints of forming, allies you want to enlist, and other interns you find attractive—all very important. Now, wait, are you smiling? Smile! We're just getting started!

THE CHAIN OF COMMAND | CHAPTER 9

 WHEN YOU'RE AN INTERN, EVERY PERSON YOU COME ACROSS IS TECHNICALLY YOUR BOSS, AND IS DEFINITELY MAKING MORE MONEY THAN YOU ARE, which keeps things simple. Remember, you signed up to be the lowest man on the totem pole, so don't get sensitive when people treat you like you don't exist.

People don't come with a strict set of rules. But in general, treat every single employee, from top to bottom, with exactly the same level of respect. Once you get to know people, you can begin to be a little more down-to-earth and a little less, shall we say, mannered, than the first few days. But use your best judgment. If you can't figure out that after a while you probably won't have to address the blunt-smoking mail guy in the same manner you'll use to talk to the woman who's just become CEO, then you're hopeless. Really.

However, you never know. Maybe the mailroom guy is more uptight than the CEO! Now what? No matter what, address the people in the mailroom politely. They probably get a lot of people who make them feel like dogs day in and day out. So approach them with, "Hi. I'm John and I just started working here as an intern, so I guess I'll be down here a lot, huh?" Maybe you'll make a friend, maybe he'll look at you like you're out of your mind. Either way, all that matters is how you handle yourself.

Next, the anchor of any company: the receptionist. Be very careful with this one. The receptionist is at the root of every phone call, envelope, and rumor that circulates through the office. If you rub the receptionist the wrong way, he or she will be sure to let everyone know. Be casual. You never know just how sly receptionists are, but since they have to deal with all kinds of people all day, just be polite, saying, "Hi, I'm John, the new intern. I hear you're in charge around here, so I wanted to make sure I got on your good side early on!" Hopefully you'll get a laugh.

Then there are the assistants. Assistants are very complicated. Some assistants are only one step above you; they just completed an internship or graduated and got an entry-level position. This means that while they will also be able to understand where you're at in your life, they can either be totally sympathetic to that or act holier-than-thou because they're finally paid employees. So remember to address assistants with a high level of respect, even though they're close to you in age. If you say "Good morning. I'm John, the new intern. It's great to meet you," and they say, "Yeah, what up, man," you can transform back into yourself so they don't think you're snotty or uptight. On the other hand, if they respond by saying, "Hello, John, it's a pleasure to meet you as well," go with it. Always treat people with whatever tone they treat you. Unless, of course, they're totally rude to you, in which case you have no choice but to suck it up and move on.

The most important person to forge a strong working relationship with is your supervisor. In most internships, you'll report to one person. You want to get to know that person, but more important, you want him or her to get to know you. Take it slow and don't push it. But try to let your supervisor know that you take your internship seriously, so that you have an ally when you need one.

Most likely, your internship supervisor will be on your side and will be easy to talk to, so you can relax a bit when dealing with him or her. From the opening handshake, be yourself, rather than trying to impress them. Internship supervisors are sort of like advisors in high school or college. Yes, your supervisor is your superior, but he or she also wants to know the real you. Don't be too cautious or tight-lipped. Your supervisor is there to be your confidant in terms of work-related issues, so take advantage of that. Just make sure he or she knows from the beginning that you're smart, confident, and willing to learn. When you have questions, turn to your supervisor first.

Here's an example of how you should introduce yourself to everyone, from managers to CEOs.

With your hand stuck out and ready to give a firm—but not overbearing—handshake, you say, "Hi, I'm John. I just started my internship here today, and I wanted to come over and introduce myself. Please let me know if there's anything I can help you with." That's it. Nothing more, nothing less.

Hint: If the person just shakes your hand and smiles, smile back and walk away. If someone says something condescending, but seemingly meant to be funny, chuckle—then walk away. Don't stop and chat with people who clearly don't want to stop or chat or you'll become the intern who everybody avoids for fear of never being able to escape you once you start talking. And if someone makes a point to talk to you, be sure to be yourself and take the time to talk to them.

Don't be nervous or scared; just have normal conversations, like you would with any adult. Above all, you should be ready for anything. You're going to be asked the "what's your major" type question on an hourly basis, so don't overthink things. No one's going to ask you a question you won't have the answer to, or say something that you won't be able to comprehend. And if that does happen, be a human being! Say, "I'm sorry, what do you mean?" Or do what most people do: smile, laugh a little, and keep it movin'.

 "HEY, DUDE!" —KARA

I showed up the Wednesday I was to begin my new internship and said hello to the woman who had interviewed me, and she said it was time for me to meet the supervisors I would be working with directly. So she took me through a few double-paned glass doors and up a flight of stairs, and led me into a large room with a few open desk areas, all occupied by men.

She introduced me to the first three older gentlemen, and when we got to the last guy, he looked much younger, and pretty hip. So I figured I'd act my damn age—and besides, he was ridiculously hot! Instead of saying, "Hello, pleased to meet you," as I had to the three other men in the room, I said, simply, "Hey, dude!"

His jaw practically dropped to the floor. I honestly thought he saw a strange figure hovering behind me, or that his jaw had just locked in the open position. Boy, was I wrong.

"'Hey, dude'?" he scoffed, staring at me with fiery eyes and flaring nostrils. "Who do you think you're talking to here? One of your friends?"

Flabbergasted, I searched for the right words but just burst into tears and muttered a few incomprehensible words like, "I, well, I didn't, sorry, sir . . ."

"Excuse us," he said, pulling the internship coordinator aside.

I was panicked. I couldn't believe I'd actually called him "dude"! I gathered myself and waited patiently for the pair to return. However, a few moments later, the door was flung open, only to reveal the internship coordinator, with "the dude" nowhere to be seen. She asked that I come into her office so we could talk.

"Listen, sweetie, I don't know how to break this to you, so I'll just come out and say it. The guy you just called 'dude' is our president and founder, Mr. Jacobs."

I sat listening, not even attempting to speak. I think I was in true shock. Not the kind of shock you feel when you find out that your ex-boyfriend just started dating your close friend, but rather the kind when you actually feel physically impaired—frozen—unable to move a muscle.

She continued, "Mr. Jacobs is an unforgiving man. In fact, he might be considered among the devil's servants, if you ask certain people."

"So what does that mean? I was just trying to be cute and sweet, I swear it!" I said, tears streaming down my face yet again.

"Honey, he says that he won't have an intern who acts like she's a child in his office. And besides, he hates sweet people, and cuteness is irrelevant because Mr. Jacobs is as gay as they come."

I couldn't believe it! How could they fire me before I'd even started? I asked the internship coordinator all these questions. I even mentioned her friendship with my internship director at school who had set this up for me.

Her response: "Sorry. I'd avoid calling employers 'dude' if I were you. Good luck."

And that was it.

MOST LIKELY YOU'LL HAVE FELLOW INTERNS. OBVIOUSLY, YOU WANT TO BE AS NORMAL AS POSSIBLE AROUND YOUR PEERS, BUT KEEP IN MIND that your fellow interns might be vying for the same position you'll be applying for down the road, so there might be some competitiveness along with the camaraderie.

When you're first introduced to other interns, play nice. You'll ask each other a bunch of questions that on one level have meaningless answers, and on another level are revealing. Questions such as:

- What's your major?
- Why are you interning at this company?
- Do you want to work in this industry later on?

Hopefully these will be pleasant, professional relationships. If you are so competitive that you need to know every intern inside and out, you may want to chill out. You're all in the same boat, so if you work well together, you'll stay afloat.

Socially, interning is unbelievable practice for the real world. You'll have to learn what to say and what not to say, and whether people you think are your friends are actually just trying to get ahead. You'll find that sharing the experience of the workplace with someone can lead to a really strong friendship.

Eventually the conversation will graduate to sociocentric questions like:

- Do you go out much?
- Are you dating anyone?
- What's your favorite club?

When it's a male/female dynamic, these questions are code for:

- Are you available?
- No, really, are you available?
- Where can I find you on weekends?

If it's a female/female dynamic, these questions are code for:

- You think you know what's cool?
- Is your boyfriend as much of a loser as you are?
- Oh, you think you know about clubs, huh?

If it's a male/male dynamic, these questions are code for:

- You're such a dork, do you ever leave the house?
- Have you ever even kissed a girl?
- Wait, on second thought, can you get me into that new spot this weekend?

There's no need to be paranoid, but bear in mind that some interns and assistants are more competitive than others. So be social, be yourself, but you might not want to reveal that you've done jail time for trafficking narcotics, or even that you hate your boss. Gossip spreads in an office like fire in a forest, so best to let your most private thoughts stay that way.

DID YOU THINK YOUR FIRST DAY WAS OVER? MR. MOLDOUN IS CALLING YOU! YOU WALK UP TO HIM EAGERLY, BUT NOT LIKE A PUPPY APPROACHING A massive bowl of Purina—more like a cat calmly approaching its bowl of water: smart, calm, and grateful. Moldoun says he wants you to get IT on the phone and get yourself set up with an e-mail account and fill out some simple forms. IT, IT, IT . . . what is that again? Right, it's office jargon for the technical people who handle your e-mail accounts and the office computer systems. You ask, "What's their extension?"

He tells you, and you pick up the phone. You give them your information and set up your account. The moment you finish, you inform Mr. Moldoun that your account is set up and you are ready to roll. He says, "Great," and walks away. You find your cubicle and keep asking people if they need help until you're blue in the face.

You talk to other interns and start getting the juice and getting to know them. You ask them every question imaginable about how things work around here. You go to lunch with them and get to know them more.

Lunch is over. Mr. Moldoun has his first project for you. He hands you a stack of paperwork and asks you to organize them first in chronological order, and then in alphabetical order. You think, *Wouldn't it make more sense to do it the other way around?* Yes, it would. You say, "Right away." You do it the way he told you to do it. When you've completed it, you say, "Mr. Moldoun, would it bother you if next time I did it the other way around? It seemed like I might have completed it a bit quicker that way."

The reasonable Mr. Moldoun says, "Sure. Whatever works best for you."

The stubborn Mr. Moldoun says, "Absolutely not. Just do what I asked you to do."

Okay, it's nearly five o'clock, and guess what? You've made it through your first day! Your stomach is finally settling and the sweat pouring profusely off your brow has tapered off a bit when Mr. Moldoun begins to make the slow walk toward your cubicle like a manager about to remove a pitcher from the mound. He finally reaches you, peers down at you for a moment, and says, "Good job today. We'll see you bright and early tomorrow."

It's over. You did it.

"THE WORST FIRST DAY IN HISTORY" —COREY

The setting: the scorching summer heat of Atlanta, Georgia—at a major investment banking firm.

Me: Nineteen years old, male, from the Northeast, an economics major.

I was lucky. I had landed a prestigious summer internship with a two-hundred-dollar weekly stipend at a well-respected investment bank that had a reputation for using interns as trainees, lending much promise to my future.

So as May came to an end and all my college buddies went home for the summer, I was about to embark on a journey into the future and beyond. I was prepared—I thought. I had one car, eight suits, three roommates, two hundred bucks a week, and potential, potential, potential.

Just after seven o'clock on the night before my first day, a few people came over to visit my female roommate. They were three cute girls so I hung out for a little while, had a beer or two, and retired up to my room just after eleven o'clock.

Around midnight, I was jolted out of my sleep by the tantalizing thumping of the sound system from the living room. I kept my cool. I wanted to go down and scream as loud as I could, considering everyone knew damn well that I had a big day tomorrow. Instead, I calmly walked downstairs and asked John, one of my roommates, if he could turn it down a notch. He agreed with an unnecessary apology to boot, but when I looked into our kitchen, I saw fifteen or twenty random kids standing in line to do keg stands. Great. Just what I needed: a night of being kept up until the wee hours by a bunch of idiots with nothing to do.

Eventually came daybreak and the start of my new gig. I went to take a shower around seven (I was due to work at nine and had a twenty-five-minute drive), and after picking a ninety-pound girl up out of the shower and placing her on the floor, I began to run the water. As the water hit my face, I noticed this strange stench coming from God knows where. Then my eyes adjusted to the day, and I found brown, thick, probably poisonous water streaming out of the shower at the speed of light. I nearly threw up at the thought of what I had just been covered in.

With no time to yell or cleanse myself any further, I just got dressed and ran out of the house. When I got to my driveway, I found my car blocked in by a squadron of SUVs.

"Somebody move these damn cars or I'll kill you people!" I screamed.

Somehow my tirade led to rapid movement, and I was out of the driveway by about seven forty-five—plenty of time to get a quick bite to eat and still be early. As I approached a light, I tapped the brake, only to feel a substantial jerk in the car, but I ignored it and kept going. Two blocks later, my right foot slowly moved over toward the brake pedal, and when I depressed it, it felt and sounded like the bludgeoning of a large farm animal. My brakes—though they allowed me to come to a full stop— were shot.

Luckily, I was right in front of a gas station. So I pulled the old Nova in and told the guy that I had to go immediately and that I'd call him during the day to discuss the price of repairs and such. I called myself a cab and figured I'd just have to go without food for the morning—no biggie.

When the cab pulled up to the office, it was actually about two minutes to nine; my planning had worked. I had left just enough time to suffer two to four major catastrophes and *still* make it to my first day on time. So I thanked my driver, gave him a nice tip, and stepped out of the cab . . . directly into the deepest puddle of mud the planet Earth has ever housed.

So although I was on time, I was also knee-high in mud, I looked like I hadn't slept in days (which was basically true), I hadn't eaten or even drunk water all morning, and, to top it off, I was nervous as hell. Muddy suit and all, I continued up the front steps into the office building. I opened the door and reached the security desk. Before I could get a word out, the guard said, "Listen, boy, I ain't got enough time in my day or money in my wallet to waste either on you. Now go out and get a job or somethin'."

I gotta tell you, I saw his point. All around me were well-groomed, fast-moving, clean, pleasant-smelling businesspeople. And I walked in with a backpack, a muddy pant leg, baggy eyes, smelling like the sewage system—what could I have expected? Nonetheless, I was five minutes late and had to get upstairs quickly.

"Um, actually, I'm here to start an internship," I said.

"What?" the guard replied with great surprise. "With who?"

"Mr. Chambers," I said.

Without uttering a word, the heavyset old Southern guard burst into uproarious laughter and somewhere in there managed to mumble, "Fifth floor, son. Chambers! Good luck, kid! See ya on the unemployment line!"

Again, I saw his point.

I went upstairs and was sent home, but luckily, Mr. Chambers was understanding enough to let me start over the next day. And the second first day turned out to be pretty good.

PART III │ HOW TO BE THE PERFECT INTERN

MAKE YOURSELF KNOWN | CHAPTER 12

 WHILE YOU'RE IN THE EARLY STAGES OF AN INTERN-SHIP, YOU HAVE TO MAKE YOURSELF KNOWN AND START TO STICK OUT FROM THE CROWD WITH ALL your hard work and appealing personality, but you also need to relax. People really won't have a sense of which interns are strongest in the first few weeks, so don't get frustrated when they don't immediately realize how smart you are. Be patient and take some initiative. There may be no better way to show what you're capable of than taking things into your own hands whenever possible.

Social adeptness is hard enough to master even without the awkward setting of an office in which you are a peon. You have to be professional. You don't want to lie, but if you're a guy, and your forty-five-year-old female supervisor asks what you did last night, it's probably best not to reply that you went out until five o'clock in the morning and woke up next to a gorgeous blonde whose name escapes you.

When given the opportunity, tell as much about yourself as you can without sharing any real juice. Talk about your goals, your aspirations, your past, your education, your family if it's called for; things of that nature. The more that people know about you, the more you'll come to mind when projects arise. The goal here is to make yourself stick out like a sore thumb—in a good way, not in the *My Cousin Vinny* kind of way.

For example, if your internship is in marketing, and a project manager knows that you have a strong interest in cars, when they are trying to market a new car, they'll come to you. They may only come to you for a lot of tedious research, but there's also a chance that your opinion will be needed.

FYI: Companies rely on interns not only for slave labor, but to stay in touch with the country's youth—what they're wearing, what they're listening to, what they're reading, and what they want when they get up in the morning.

Remember, people don't just give out internships to help you—they need your help! It's not just free work they need these days; companies need your opinion, your vision, and your youthful zest for life! So don't be timid when a situation you can help with arises.

A great way to begin letting people know how fabulous you are is to interject small bits of knowledge when it's appropriate. So if you hear a bunch of employees trying to remember the name of an actor they want to work with and you know who they're talking about, just politely say, "Oh, you mean Brian Dennehy. Hell of an actor. I particularly liked him in *F/X2*. He was also great in *Death of a Salesman* on

Broadway." Don't act like a know-it-all, just a well-informed young person. This way, people will remember that you're actually a person, not just a faxing wizard who occasionally makes a lovely cup of coffee. You gotta take the risk. More than likely, people will respond to your knowledge with acceptance and appreciation rather than spite and resentment.

This is another reason why you have to be hyperaware of your office's employees. If you think the guy in that corner cubicle is the type that truly looks at interns as peons, just avoid him, and don't try to usurp him in any way, whether it's with your knowledge, your work ethic, or your dashing good looks. Just stay away from him and do what he says. If you're always doing exactly what you're told, even the shallowest, most spiteful guy in the office will have no choice but to respect you, at least on a surface level. Some people will never give you a chance, but that's out of your control, and you should never attempt to seek help from those people or help the ones who obviously don't want to help you.

Don't worry about those people; in ten years, when your four internships and close reading of *The Intern Files* have catapulted you to the top of the food chain, the same guy will want a job from you, and you'll be in the position to say, "Remember me, buddy?" Even in the wonderful world of interning, what goes around, comes around—eventually.

"THEY KNOW HER FOR ALL THE WRONG REASONS" —TIM

So you're supposed to make yourself known, right? Right. However, you have to be known for the right reasons. I worked for a well-known publishing house in New York, and one summer we had this intern— I'll call her Kristen—who made it a point to wear as many revealing outfits as she could.

I was an assistant editor at the time, so I had frequent contact with the interns—especially Kristen. Every day I got to know her body better and better. No, not because I'm some slime-ball who was looking to exploit young girls, but because her outfits got skimpier every day. One day she'd wear a see-through shirt with no bra, the next a miniskirt with no underwear.

So she became known as "the tramp," rather than Kristen. I'm a guy, so I can't say I didn't notice, but the way she degraded herself on a daily basis was shameless and feeble. To be honest with you, I felt bad for the kid. So one day I pulled her aside and tried to talk to her about the matter.

"Kristen," I said, "I know you like to wear, uh, slightly edgy clothing, but I don't think it's appropriate in the office, particularly for an intern."

She gazed at me for a moment and said, "You're right, I need to start *doing* rather than just *showing*!"

It took me a moment, but when I realized what she meant, I implored her to think again. "Kristen, listen. I think you may have the wrong idea."

"Wrong idea?" she said, cutting me off promptly. "We both know how to get on the express elevator to the top of the business world."

"Kristen, do you really want yourself to be looked at like some kind of object?"

"If it gets me a corner office, I don't really care!"

And that was it. Kristen took off down the hall.

Her outfits got skimpier and skimpier, and rumors began to fly around the office about one-night stands she was having with higher-ups. But then one day when I was leaving work, I saw Kristen sitting with her head in her hands on the steps outside.

"Kristen," I said softly, "what's the matter?"

With a faint smile she looked up. "You were right. Everyone knew who I was, and I thought everyone liked me. But I just got fired because I tried to kiss Mr. Smith at happy hour last night. He said that I was finished," she explained, holding back tears.

IT'S SIMPLE, IT'S BASIC, BUT IT'S ESSENTIAL. ABOVE ALL, THE SINGLE MOST IMPORTANT ASPECT OF INTERNING IS DOING ALL THE WORK THAT IS assigned to you and doing it well. Naturally, there will be times when you try and fail, but any employer would rather see you give it your best shot than not do it at all. This means that you can never forget or choose not to do something for any reason. If you can't figure something out, or if you have any questions at all, ask your supervisor or whoever has given you the assignment. If you're too busy to take on a particular assignment, even though you really want it, you have to be up-front about that. Tell the person who gave you the assignment that you'd love to do it, but since you're so busy, you need a week or so to finish it. They may say yes, they may give the assignment to someone else, but either outcome is better than getting in over your head and not turning something in on time.

If you do find yourself in over your head and swamped with work, again, talk to your supervisor. As long as you're honest about what's going on with your workload, you're doing the right thing. When you attempt to do too much, even if it's well intended, you'll find yourself swamped and causing other employees additional stress—which is exactly what you're *not* there to do. So if you see that you have three projects due on Tuesday, and you know that you won't be able to finish all three, talk to the project heads and describe the situation, and suggest that they enlist someone else's help or ask for an extension. Let your supervisor decide what to do.

However, even though it happens, you should do your best to stay out of situations where you end up swamped. A great way to avoid such situations is to keep a running list of all assignments you have. You may be an intern, but you'll also find that if you're performing well, you'll get as much work as some real employees, which means that you need to be just as responsible as the people who do get paid to do their jobs. There might be times when you *think* you can juggle six projects at once, and it turns out that you can only handle four. Always follow this simple rule: Never try to rush something to compensate for your lack of time. Always be honest with your supervisor.

As long as you stick to that rule, you'll be fine. But there will probably be times when you overestimate yourself, and when that happens, you must be prepared to admit it. Things can only turn out badly if you try to cover up the fact that you may be in over your head. Employers are looking for people who not only do all their work on time, but know how to deal with it when they foresee problems arising. So get all your work done as best you can, and have the courage to admit it when you think you may be headed for trouble.

"MONDAY ALWAYS COMES." —JEN

How seriously did I take my internship in the Ad Sales Research department of a major television network in NYC? On most levels, I took it as seriously as any real job, or an informative college course that I (my parents) was paying for. I arrived on time or early on most days. I took in all the hands-on experience, office culture, and knowledge I could, and completed all tasks I was given in a timely manner. In fact, I went above and beyond the call of duty each and every chance I had. I was respected—I thought—like a real employee.

You're not really *expected* to treat internships as real jobs—but if you're serious about the field/department/company you are currently with, you damn well better. What I learned (the tough way) was just how worklike an internship really is. The better and more respected you are, the more that will be expected of you in terms of professionalism.

One day while I was at my internship, I got a call from my mom explaining that my grandmother was not going to make it through the night, and I needed to get home as soon as possible. She had been sick, and I knew that, but naturally I panicked, began to tear up, and went to find my supervisor to tell him I had to leave. He was very understanding if a bit taken aback, and he told me to go take care of everything I had to do. I told him I would be in touch and left to book my flight.

Needless to say, my internship was one of the last things on my mind while dealing with a very difficult and long week of endless services and other forms of mourning. When I was finally able to return to New York, my mom accompanied me to help me settle back in. That Monday, one of the first things I did when I came back was call my internship supervisor.

I didn't have contact with the office for the week I was gone; however, I figured my supervisor would be more than understanding of my situation considering the circumstances. When I called, I got a totally insensitive response coupled with a tone-de-disappointment; something to the effect of, "Well, I hadn't heard from you in a while . . . and we didn't know if you were coming back. . . ." I was floored, hurt, and angry. I told him I was sorry that I had not reached out to him earlier and that this was my first day back in the city. I explained that the process was not easy and filled him in on the details—details I felt I shouldn't have even needed to provide in the first place, but particularly considering the strict timeline of traditional burial and ceremonies that come along with the Orthodox faith—all of which he knew full well, since he was Jewish too.

I went in the next day to speak with my supervisor face-to-face, and all I took away from the conversation was the hard-learned lesson that no matter what the circumstance, in order to make it in the real world, you have to keep your employer abreast with your situation so long as your mouth and voice box are both intact. Being a Super Intern means people will actually start to treat you with respect, and more importantly, they will expect the same level of respect and professionalism in return. Anyway, while trying to express his concern, all I really got from my supervisor were questions as to why he had not heard from me; while I felt hurt and taken aback by his attitude, his point made an impact on me that I'll never forget.

He essentially made me understand that one always needs to check in and can't leave anyone hanging, no matter what type of a position you think you're in (even a lowly intern). He even explained that when his superiors came to inquire as to where I was, he didn't know what to say, other than that there had been a death in the family two weeks earlier and he hadn't heard from me since, which he said made him look bad too. Even though he told them that my grandmother had passed away two weeks earlier, that wasn't good enough for the three major employees who needed an intern's help on three equally as major projects. His points were valid and taught me an important lesson.

While I still look back at the situation with mixed emotions, I realize that my supervisor was right, and I will always remember his advice. As he put it, "You can't hide forever—Monday always comes."

BELIEVE IT OR NOT, AT SOME POINT IN YOUR LIFE, YOU'LL *WANT* TO BE BUSY. IT MAY NOT BE TODAY, BUT WHEN YOU FIND YOURSELF STUCK IN A CUBICLE for forty hours a week with nothing to do, AOL Instant Messenger will get old. How many times a day can you and your friends talk about how boring work is and how wasted you're going to get later that night? Sure, that's always at least mildly appealing, but it won't fill up forty hours.

As you are aware, companies sometimes don't know how to make use of their interns in an efficient way. But this definitely doesn't mean that you should ever slack off. So if you find yourself constantly being told that there's nothing for you to do, you have to learn to take initiative.

Once you get a sense of who might really be a good person to get to know, ask that person more frequently if he or she needs anything. This is called the walk-around. When there is nothing to do, you're not doing your job. There's always *something* to do. If there's a moment when your supervisor says he or she has nothing for you, walk through the office and ask people if they need help with anything. Start with the people who you think really want to use interns for more in-depth work; that way you can show them what you're capable of, not just how quickly you can make copies. It'll only take a little while for you to figure out who wants to help you and who wants to enslave you.

If you really enjoy a particular project, make that known. For example, if you worked on some Internet-based research and you actually liked it, tell your supervisor, "Just so you know, I really enjoyed researching all those new cars and their demographics today. If you ever have a similar project, I'd love to help you out again." By showing a touch of enthusiasm, you'll increase the chances of your name popping into someone's head when they need something done.

But you have to start slow. Never try to go too far above and beyond in your first few weeks. Slowly acclimate yourself to your surroundings and the work at hand before you attempt to become Super Intern. If you attempt to stretch yourself too thin, there's a good chance you'll falter a bit. You have to really know the environment and the politics of your office before you try to take it to the next level.

After a few weeks have passed, you'll learn that working hard means being at least slightly annoying. Your coworkers might have thought you were a pain in the ass the first four times you asked if you could help out, but when they finally needed help, they remembered that annoying intern. That's when you get to prove what you're capable of. By next week, you'll have a corner office—definitely!

Once you've successfully annoyed every employee in the building (this includes, but is not limited to, everyone from the janitor to the CEO), do whatever kind of mindless work your company needs. You know, jobs like updating databases and press clippings. However, press clippings can only be done once a day, and the database is only as large as the company, so you might have to get creative.

Check to see that all equipment within the department that you're interning for is running well. Does the printer need paper? Are any computers down? Are the fax machines actually sending and receiving, or are they making erratic, bizarre noises because there's something wrong with them?

Check on supplies. Does anyone need more pens? What about file folders? Is Andy's desk a complete mess? Politely ask him if he needs some file folders or envelopes. Check the supply closet, if there is one—what needs to be refilled? Paper, glue, air filters (hey, you never know)? Refill these without asking. Go to the company's main supply room and get what's needed. If you need to go and buy a few things, tell your supervisor that you need paper and ask for some petty cash so you can go out and get it. Your effort will be appreciated—sometimes—or at least occasionally.

File cabinets are always a great place to spend some meaningless time. Wherever you work, it is inevitable that there will be at least one cabinet or area that is loaded with files, which need to be alphabetized, placed in chronological order, and organized. That cabinet, drawer, or area will be the area that everyone else avoids, so people will definitely notice if you organize it.

When in doubt: Clean! Honestly, there may be nothing that employees appreciate more than interns who aren't above doing a little dirty work. As an intern, it's your job to embark on the tasks that others don't have time to deal with. Getting your hands dirty is always appreciated. Clean up conference rooms, your intern area, wherever—

so long as you're not fiddling with other peoples' personal materials.

Usually a company's interns share an area or a few cubicles; clean and organize them! Make them look perfect so that when there is actually real work to do, it can be done without having to get supplies or straighten up your desk.

If there really doesn't seem to be anything in the entire office that you can either help with, take care of, clean, organize, brew, or scrub, just get on your computer and do something to look busy—in a work-related way, obviously. Research within the area or field that your company deals with. Maybe you'll stumble onto information that your company can use at some point.

If you work in the music industry, research relevant artists. Maybe a few weeks later, your company will want to work with an artist who you researched, and you'll be able to blow away a few people with how much you already know about that artist. If you work for a media outlet, research and recommend potential stories. Maybe they'll use them, maybe they won't. Can't hurt. If you work for any kind of financial group, be aware of exactly what's going on with the market that day.

The point is that there is never *nothing* to do. If you find yourself using your spare time to nap, eat, chat, or view things online that you should save for your personal time, you're either not working hard enough, or there's really no reason for you to be there. Why aren't you working hard enough? If it's because you're a slacker, keep slacking off and see where it gets you. If it's because you despise your internship, address that issue with your school and see if it's too late to make a change. If you've tried everything in your power to make work for yourself, and you *still* can't find anything to do, you probably are at a company that doesn't need you, in which case you should have a formal meeting with your internship supervisor to discuss the matter. It's perfectly possible that they haven't realized you've exhausted all the things to do.

"THE ART OF SUCKING IT UP" —LUCY

My first real internship was at a magazine where I'd become their most trusted intern, and where I think I was very well liked. However, I eventually began to overstep my boundaries, and one day I really screwed up. We were orchestrating an event at a local venue for a big-name clothing line, and the people at my magazine wanted to set up a hot dog stand outside, and a roaming pizza server inside, to give the party a sort of all-American feel. (God, this sounds so unbelievably absurd and meaningless in retrospect!) Anyhow, I told my boss that I would handle both areas myself. I had other projects to handle and was given few details, as usual.

Here's where I went wrong. As I went on my hunt for the perfect hot dog vendor and pizza man to serve the eight-hour event, I would call the office, ask for details in terms of budget, and either not get an answer or not be called back at all. However, at the end of each day, my boss would say, "Oh, don't worry, we have time, do it tomorrow," and instead of pressing her, I simply sat back and took my time (i.e., sucked it up). Exactly one week before the event was to happen, I had a famous New York pizzeria waiting for the contract, but no hot dog man. As I entered the office that morning, a friend said that he had overheard my supervisor being berated by her boss for being so disorganized. Furthermore, he said that my boss then proceeded to lay blame on me and me alone, for which she was then nearly fired for entrusting the lowly intern with such responsibility (pizza and hot dogs!). Anyway, I walked right into this shitstorm, which proceeded to boisterously break loose.

So I'm sitting there listening to these two tell me repeatedly that it's entirely my fault, the party could fall apart because of me, and well . . . it might be the end of the world, too! All I had to do to save my own ass was explain that the only reason things hadn't yet been finalized was because my direct superior wouldn't respond to any of my budget questions, and that had she done so, we would have been ready to go weeks before. But I didn't. So the meeting ended with both of us "in trouble," and my supervisor and I literally never said another pleasant word to each other again. Did she simply get caught being totally unprepared and subsequently blame the whole ordeal on me, or did she intentionally let me go through this whole process blindly so that I would inevitably fail? I'll never know. But what I do know is that I sucked it up to the point of hurting myself. While interns must always be respectful, they must never be taken advantage of. Because taking advantage of an intern is easy. From that day on, I never once allowed myself to be taken advantage of in any situation—I just approached every potential issue with caution and class.

DON'T GET TAKEN ADVANTAGE OF | CHAPTER 15

 YOU MIGHT FIND YOURSELF DOING FAR TOO MUCH AT YOUR INTERNSHIP. SOMETIMES IT'S HARD TO KNOW IF YOU'RE BEING TAKEN ADVANTAGE OF.

Is your bank charging you unnecessary fees? Does your local video store owner charge *you* the same price he charges longtime customers for a one night rental? Is your credit card company's latest scam a little worse than another company's scam? Are taxes really *this* high? Yes! Is it okay for your boss to ask you to drop her dry cleaning off after office hours without even offering train fare? Ah, now *that* is not so easy to answer!

No matter what you're asked to do, no matter how ridiculous it seems, no matter how much it resembles yesterday's task, do it. At least, that is, unless you think you're being taken for a ride. While most companies *use* their interns, some *abuse* them. Sometimes you'll be asked to do things that seem pointless or boring; other times you'll be asked to do things that just don't make sense. As long as these things are within office hours and don't require the human body to stretch beyond reasonable measures, you have two choices: do it, or do it really well. You can choose not to do it, but that's a great way to have your internship terminated immediately.

First, since you're probably not getting paid, you have to make sure that you aren't actually *paying* to work for a company. Every time you are asked to leave the work site, even if you'll only need a few dollars for the subway, never be afraid to speak up and ask your supervisor how you can get reimbursed for travel expenditures. If you are working for no monetary compensation, there is no reason that you should ever have to dole out even a penny of your own, particularly if you are running someone else's errand. Depending on geography, you may even score a company car, but don't hold your breath.

It is commonplace to have interns do strange things. In fact, more often than not, you'll be doing things that you really don't understand the purpose of. Unfortunately, you have no leverage whatsoever, so it's not really your place to ask questions about why you have been given an assignment. Remember: You're an intern. But if you're being asked to do something that you will have an allergic reaction to, something illegal, or something that cuts into your studies or even your personal life, you're most likely being taken advantage of.

The line between what's acceptable and what's abusive can be hard to see, and ultimately you're the only person who can decide where it is. You may be willing to do things the next guy or gal isn't. On one hand, this gives you a leg up. On the other hand, you may fall victim to becoming overworked and underpaid before you even get a paycheck. Remember, since you're an intern, you don't get overtime and you won't be seeing a December bonus to help you install that new pool in your backyard. In other words, only do what you feel comfortable with, and don't be afraid to make it known when you feel like you're getting jerked around.

Endless filing, faxing, and coffee making most definitely does not qualify as getting jerked. Running errands on a hot day doesn't either. However, being asked, as the office is closing, to drop off someone's dry cleaning on your way home is the first level of getting jerked. If you leave at six every day, and someone asks you to run a personal errand for them when you're halfway out the door, say yes only if you truly have the time, the money, and the freedom to do it. If you have something important to do, respectfully say, "I'm sorry, I have to get home to write this paper as soon as I can and I don't have any extra time to spare."

You may just have dinner plans that you really can't miss. If the person who asked the favor of you is someone you feel comfortable with, tell them the truth. However, if you have no relationship with this person, you might want to stick with the paper thing. Don't totally lie, just bend the truth a bit and mention the words "school" and "paper." This is a judgment call that you'll have to make on your own. You don't want to weave a web of lies that's too tangled to keep up with, but you also don't want to seem lazy, so you'll have to make that choice on the spot. Honesty is always the best policy, of course, but when you're an intern, some folks may not respond to the "dinner plans" approach too well.

It's important to separate doing personal favors from doing work-related, essential errands. If you're asked to do something last-minute for the betterment of your company, you should do it immediately and not be the least bit resentful about it. If it costs you a few dollars, ask for reimbursement the next day, not as soon as you return. However, when it starts to become personal, try to be sure that you are not being taken advantage of by someone. If anyone tries to intimidate you or bully you into doing things for them that don't feel legit to you, tell your supervisor immediately. If it's the intern supervisor making you stretch beyond your limits, tell your internship advisor at school and he or she will probably help you deal with it.

How do you figure out when you're being taken advantage of and when you're simply at an internship that sucks? It's tough, and you can't administer a lie-detector test every time you feel like saying, "Are you doing this to get out of it yourself? Do you just hate me?" Unfortunately, all you can do is everything you're asked to do, even if it's grudgingly, and discuss with your school advisor each specific incident in which you felt like you may have been getting pushed around. Get your advisor's advice for every situation on a case-by-case basis. Don't forget, companies often don't know what to do with their interns, so you may think people are pushing you around, taking advantage of you, or just continually giving you monotonous work, when really they just don't know what else to do with you.

Knowing your limits is really important. For example, if you have a night class, and you're continually being asked to stay at your internship until eight when you were initially told that your day would end at six, you're being pushed too hard and need to stand up for yourself. Approach your supervisor and explain the situation calmly and reasonably. Don't whine and complain, even if that's what you really feel like doing. Do not be uppity at all—you need to be professional, even if you've been treated unfairly.

The only thing you can do is address the situation and hope that your supervisor understands. If he or she doesn't, you should turn to your school for help. Perhaps the company has a Human Resources department. They might be able to help you too. Even if you feel like yelling and screaming at your supervisor, or even just talking back, bite your tongue until you can bring it up with your school's internship director, or HR, and let them help you. Taking things into your own hands is great in terms of being known for your initiative—like getting projects started on your own—but if there's a political issue of some sort, you might want to involve a third party. That's what they're there for, and you'll probably need some backup.

You may run into a different situation: You really wish you could stay until eight, but you can't because of school. Yes, it's great to put in the extra effort if you don't mind and if you can afford to do so. But school has to come first. Don't feel like you're missing out on opportunities because you have to get to class. Your company will understand that.

There are also times when a company will hire too many interns in one semester, leaving a shortage of actual work. This often leads to supervisors coming up with meaningless work to kill time. The result is that when there is actual work to be done, your time has been used up doing trivial things, perhaps leaving you with an hour to do real work that is going to take you three hours. You can't say no to the real work, but at the same time, you may feel overwhelmed. The only choice you have is to do what you've been asked as well as you can, and work until you absolutely have to leave. You may know that the mistake was on the supervisor's part, but they know it too, so don't rub it in.

Another common situation is that some companies just can't figure out how to really utilize their interns and then end up overworking them. For example, let's say the company you're interning for is having a party on a Tuesday night. They want you to attend the party as a representative of the company, even though you'll have worked all day and will have to stay until ten o'clock, and be back in class or at your internship early the next morning.

The intention of sending you to the party is probably to give you something fun to do. However, since you are still an intern, you're uncomfortable, you have a miserable night, and by the time you get home, you can't write that paper for class, and you get two hours of sleep. No one is taking advantage of you here, it's just bad timing. Remember, school comes first, so you can always decline the invitation: Tell them you've got to write a paper that night!

Whether there are too many interns or not enough interns, too many on Tuesday but too few on Wednesday, you have to be very careful not to stir the pot when nothing's cooking. If you start to complain when there's really nothing to complain about, you'll be looked at as immature. Just make sure you give your company the benefit of the doubt. You don't want to sabotage yourself, after all. Ask questions, stay informed, and you'll be okay. If it feels like there may be too many interns on a particular day and you're able to switch your schedule around, just say to your supervisor, "I noticed that on Tuesday there are six of us, but I always hear people complain that they're short on interns on Fridays. Would you like me to switch my days?"

If you're truly at your wit's end, your internship director is absolutely in a position to make a phone call on your behalf to inform your supervisor of the situation. So if you're in week ten of your internship and you haven't yet been able to do anything other than file and fax, alert your advisor and let him or her help you navigate it with caution. What feels like abusiveness may just be incompetence on your company's part, you may be overreacting, or you might just not be cut out for this particular internship. Before you point fingers, make sure to really think about what's going on. Consider the fact that things aren't always what they seem, and your bosses are all human too. And remember, you're an intern. Be patient—if nothing else, you'll learn how to handle your interns when you're the boss.

"NO PROBLEM. I CAN STAY TILL NINE O'CLOCK" —JEFF

I worked for this event-marketing group in Miami during my junior year. I was already a party promoter in town, so I knew the industry quite well, even for a twenty-year-old kid. In fact, I probably would have been better served not interning at all, but I wanted to see what it was like to work for a "real" marketing firm rather than just guerrilla e-mailing/calling/flyering/blabbering with my friends to fill up nightspots, only seeing a few hundred dollars a weekend after working all week.

When I started my internship, things were pretty straightforward and, frankly, rather boring, which was actually nice. I needed office experience, not just interpersonal skills. However, after about a month or so, things took a turn for the worse. One sweltering afternoon, my boss pulled me into her office to tell me that she thought it was best that my role change; I needed to take a more "hands-on approach" to the marketing world, she said.

This sounded great. I mean, the company had major clients and did major events—not just weekend club promotions with a gaggle of useless promoters who made a half million dollars a year to kiss ass for a living, which was the life I had been headed for. The company wanted me to work directly with the clients, and although it would mean longer hours, I would receive a commission based on my client intake. It sounded like a step in the right direction.

So the next day I was given a schedule of late weeknight events in the South Beach area. I was taking four classes that semester, which meant two days of class, two days of work, with Fridays off. But my classes, which fell on Tuesdays and Thursdays starting at eight thirty a.m., were the last of my requirements, which meant that falling short in any of them was absolutely out of the question. The firm I was interning for knew all of this.

So I asked my boss about this semi-important-looking schedule. I asked if I would be prepping the events in terms of getting staff organized during the day, dealing with press, or what. My boss's response was so deceptive that it was ridiculous. She said, "Oh, no, no, no. You'll be the company's main representative on the floor every night. You're young, tall, good-looking—everything people want to see when they think of our firm."

I assumed that working nights would mean that they would give me my days off. Even that would have been a challenge, since I'd be exhausted for my morning classes. But in reality, the company wanted me to come into the office on my scheduled days and then work the company's events at night, too. And guess what? I agreed to it. I wanted to prove that I could handle everything on my own.

So for a month or so I worked seven days a week, including nights and, of course, weekends. But man, did it catch up to me. I was so tired every day that I began passing out in class, and occasionally at work. I failed two major tests, lost about ten pounds, looked like the lead in *Night of The Living Dead*, and had absolutely no social life. My role at these events was to either work the door until three or four in the morning, or stand around listening to drunken employees bitch about their watered-down sex lives at home. And you know what else? I hadn't seen a dime. Commission? For what? There was no commission to be made in my role, and I was given no stipend, no bonuses—nothing. It was time to take a stand.

So one morning I marched into my boss's office and said that we needed to talk. She tried telling me she was too busy, that she didn't have any time, and a few other similar escape tactics, but out of sheer exhaustion and almost unbearable frustration, I shouted, "No! I need to talk to you now!"

We were both in shock; had I really just yelled at my boss, my supervisor, the passport to my future? I was terrified. I saw my career come to an end before it even started. Then she took a deep breath, kicked her legs up on the desk, and said, "Well, you certainly have my attention now. What is so urgent?"

Relieved, though still a bit wary of the impending doom my career would likely suffer if I didn't play my cards right, I began talking. I told her how much I wanted to be a part of the company. I told her that while I would work nights if I could, my schoolwork was suffering severely, and at this rate I probably wouldn't graduate.

I told her that financial compensation had been promised over a month before and I hadn't seen a dime. I was working weekends, days, nights; hell, I think I even worked in my sleep once!

And then I gathered myself and looked up at my boss, an attractive middle-aged woman who, at the moment, looked as if she were about to leap across her desk and disembowel me. Instead she sighed and began speaking. "You know what? You're a fool," she began. "But I must say, I admire you. I admire your work ethic, I admire your drive, and most of all, I admire your apparently gargantuan set of balls."

"Really?" I asked.

"Yes, really," she continued. "I've been pushing you beyond your capacity, and I apologize for that. I can't say I agree with the way you stormed in here, but it worked."

We talked a while longer and agreed that when I did have time, I would work the company's nightly events and be given a hundred dollars for each event. Furthermore, my boss actually admitted that she was taking advantage of me and said that she would never do it again. Maybe it was all just lip service, but I couldn't have asked for a better outcome. My only regrets were being too afraid to broach the topic sooner and letting myself be taken advantage of for so long. But it happens—regularly—and most companies just get away with it.

YOU KNOW WHAT TO WEAR. YOU KNOW HOW TO TREAT PEOPLE. YOU KNOW HOW TO WORK HARD AND HOW TO STAND UP FOR YOURSELF WHEN you're being taken advantage of. You even know how to make yourself useful when there's very little to do. In fact, you know almost all the realities that come along with interning. Now you need to know how to take it to the next level, how to go beyond what is expected of you whenever you can. This is inside information, so pay attention.

Do as you're told, do it well, be polite—that's all obvious to you by now, right? Once you've gotten the feel for things, it's time to unleash all of your powers, one by one. The key to becoming Super Intern is to seize every moment and take a few risks. When you see an opportunity—even an opportunity that seems daunting—you have to be brave enough to take it. Where others are insecure, you always have to be ready, willing, and able.

Some interns think that the way to impress employers is to be the quickest gun in the office. In truth, it's more important to be the sharpest tool in the shed, which means when it's time for you to be fast, you give them fast. When it's time to pay attention to detail and take your time, take as much time as you need to complete the project with such precision that you'll never have to hear someone tell you to "pay closer attention next time."

If you're asked for an in-depth research report, dig until you hit the bottom. If it takes you an hour to find every vital statistic and piece of information you need, fine. Then take an extra hour to organize what you've found in a way that is so clear and concise, any novice could understand it. If it takes you the whole day, that's fine too, assuming your supervisor doesn't need it immediately. So long as you've done all you could, including asking questions when needed, you'll have done a great job, while the next guy might have raced to the finish line, turning in an incomprehensible report that actually creates more work. Even if you make a mistake or two, your effort will show, and that's what will matter—even CEOs make mistakes.

On the other hand, if you're asked to do something that's time-sensitive, be sure to ask for the exact deadline. It'll help if you're already ahead of the game. This means always knowing where everything is in the office, and what everyone's names and job descriptions are. Make it a point to give yourself daily tests on peoples' names, where the backup printer is, and what people's extensions are.

You should always be aware of what people are working on. Without being nosy, politely ask employees, particularly when you're actually helping them, about the projects they're working on. People tend to give interns assignments without explaining the backstory. All you have to do is ask. You may not get an answer, but the more you know about what's going on around you, the better equipped you'll be when your number is called.

Another way to be superprepared and always do an outstanding job is to familiarize yourself with all research tactics that are available to you. Most people know about Google and 411, but does your company use Lexis Nexis? What about industry-specific Web sites and publications that are meant for, and only apply to, one particular field? If you work at a sports-related company, know how to navigate ESPN.com, MLB.com, NBA.com, like the back of your hand. Rip out the sports pages every morning to stay as informed as possible. If you work for a film company, learn about Web sites like IMDb.com and figure out how to use them efficiently. See tons of movies—from low-budget indie flicks to major blockbusters. The key is to be saturated with an almost obsessive amount of information about the company you work for and the field it's in. Most interns are just trying things out and taking it lightly. You may be doing the same, but if you want to be a Super Intern, use your spare time to go a step further, as long as you don't feel totally bogged down, stressed out, or like a complete freak.

Even though you want to be ultraprepared and as available and helpful as possible, remember to be inquisitive, not annoying. You know you're supposed to ask people for help and see what's really going on around the office, but if someone seems busy, sometimes the best thing to do is to leave them alone.

Ask a question every time you have one. If your supervisor isn't available, keep a list of questions and ask them when he or she has time to answer. The biggest mistake interns make is trying to do things on their own when they're really not sure of something. If you want that perfect research report, you'll have to begin by realizing that you're nowhere near perfect. If you have a question about something, ask it, otherwise you run the risk of making an error that will take some time to undo or redo. Unfortunately, there *are*—in some people's minds—stupid questions. So if you get a snide answer, don't be surprised or deterred. Keep asking, even if you run the risk of asking redundant questions. It's better to be redundant than to ruin a project.

Important Question: "When you said you wanted me to research the demographic Pepsi's targeting for their new campaign, which particular campaign did you mean? When will it begin? Is it for a particular beverage the company makes, or the entire brand?"
Stupid Question: "Do you think they're targeting young people?"

Important Question: "How would you like me to compile the data? Should I type out a report, e-mail it to you, or just take some notes and come and discuss them with you later?"
Stupid Question: "What font size should I use when I type up the report?"

The stupid questions are the ones that people can respond to by saying something like, "You can do that on your own," or "If I knew, I wouldn't have asked for your help," or "Is that *really* important?" While you need to know how the report should be delivered, you can't waste time on superfluous details like font size. Don't send it in boldfaced twenty-four-point font. Think about it. If your supervisor wants something that specific, he or she will probably tell you.

Important Question: "Is there anything in particular I should keep in mind while doing this project? For example, should I take particular note of how this campaign differs from others, or if Pepsi's targeting minorities more than in the past?"

Stupid Question: "So what's the point of all this?"

Surely the Super Intern in you wants to know the point, but watch your delivery. You can definitely ask if there's anything specific to look for, or anything your supervisor may have left out. But don't just come out and ask why you're being asked to do something. Just do what you're told better, with more detail, and faster than everyone else. Besides, you may want to save those questions for awkward moments when no one has anything to say in the cafeteria or in the elevator. Rest assured, there'll be more of those times than you care to imagine, and you'll definitely need the material.

To go above and beyond also means dedicating as much time to the job as you can without negatively affecting the rest of your life. If you can stay a little late once a week, make sure everyone knows that you're available. If you can come in at eight but aren't asked to be in until ten, let them know that, too. You could even send an officewide e-mail informing everyone that if they need an extra hand—or mind, as it were—you're available.

If you have information or knowledge that can help your company in general, or, come in handy for a particular assignment, don't withhold it. Maybe your company really wants to use the public library for a meeting and your mom's the librarian—call your mama and tell her how much you need her help and watch how impressed your company will be (hey, librarians impress everyone, don't they?). If your company wants to do some work with a particular art gallery and you know someone there, do everything in your power to set the two up.

The key is not to offer anything until you're sure of it. If you say, "Hey, I know someone there, maybe I can help out," and it falls through, you end up looking terrible, even if it's not your fault. Most employees will expect you to know nothing, so they'll be thoroughly impressed by any extra effort you put in, or at the very least make a mental note of it. If you work for one of those rare companies that actually expect their interns to do things like this, you'll gain more respect than you already had. The main hazard is if you do a favor for someone who then resents you for being able to do something they can't, rather than appreciating the extra work you've put in. That's just a risk you'll have to take.

Always make sure that you're not being ingratiating or irritating by trying to do something a little extra. Only look to take the next step where it's necessary. In other words, if you know John in Editorial loves two Dunkin' Donuts in the morning, don't just show up one day with a half-dozen doughnuts in hand. What do you do the next day? Bring him a dozen?

Going above and beyond is something that few people will actually want to do, but it can make all the difference in whether you get a job later. Most people are just content doing what they're supposed to. But if you strive for greatness, you're far more likely to achieve it.

PART IV | SOCIAL ETIQUETTE AT THE OFFICE

DO YOUR WORK, THEN TELL SUZIE ABOUT YOUR WEEKEND | CHAPTER 17

 HERE'S THE THING ABOUT INTERNING AND SOCIAL-IZING: WHILE YOU HOPE TO FIND A WORK ENVIRON-MENT THAT'S FRIENDLY, AND MAYBE EVEN ONE where you really vibe with your coworkers, you can never get *too* comfortable, or put socializing ahead of—or even on a par with—your work. Furthermore, your friends outside of your internship? Yeah, they don't exist until you have a free moment, or until the day is done. There are three main ways people waste time socializing at the office.

THE PHONE

Do not keep your cell phone on during internship hours, unless it's part of the job, in which case you should use it only for business. The only circumstance in which you can talk to friends is in an incredibly lax office where your supervisor clearly says that if there's nothing to do (which you know doesn't happen anyway) then you can talk to a friend for a few minutes. But if it's not offered, don't ask. If you have a lunch break and need to get in touch with a friend, do it while you chew. Period.

E-MAIL

Please don't be that intern who pretends to look busy by e-mailing or IM-ing all day. News flash: Not only will you get caught, you're wasting your own time. If that's what you want to do with yourself, do it from home. Also, if you think that IM-ing fellow interns in the office is okay, you're wrong, because someone will definitely notice that *all* their interns are IM-ing. Save it for lunch, which is the hour you should reserve for intern gossip anyhow.

STOP-AND-CHAT

Sorry folks, the time-honored office routine known as the stop-and-chat or the cube-lean is not for interns. There is maybe nothing more aggravating for employers than seeing their young, allegedly hard-working interns standing around like they're between classes. Sometimes you'll get to do projects with other interns; say you're just stuffing envelopes in a conveyor-belt formation. Feel free to talk quietly among yourselves, as long as it doesn't slow you down. Don't walk around gossiping to other interns or real employees when you can be doing something productive.

Relax: You're not in prison. There'll definitely be times that you just sit around with your coworkers or fellow interns and shoot the shit until there's no more shit to be shot. However, this happens when your boss says so. If he or she engages you, cool, hang out for a while. If you have an important e-mail from a friend to respond to, one that's not just gossip about last night, take thirty seconds and write back. But really, keep it to the bare minimum.

The point is that your work always has to come first. You have to find the right balance of hard work and taking a moment or two throughout the day to actually talk to people (i.e., remain sane). Just find a way to put your work first. Once you know what you're doing and have the respect of your employer, you'll be able to loosen the muzzle ever so slightly, but this only comes once you've proven yourself capable of always completing your tasks on time.

It's not that bad . . . just do your work already!

 ## "YOU CAN'T REALLY BE THIS NICE" —EMILY

I once interned for a monthly music magazine. There were five interns that spring. We were all there on different days, and we were quite different in terms of our goals and our personalities. When we did see each other, we interacted well, always keeping things at a superficial level. However, there was one girl, Jazmine, who was just too damn nice to be trusted. And by nice, I mean ingratiating; ingratiating toward other interns, and ingratiating toward employees, from the mail guy to the editor-in-chief.

While the other interns and a few employees seemed to buy her little act, I was suspicious from the start. She was just too pleasant and proper. She flirted with the male staff and buddied up with the female staff. She knew next to nothing about music, yet always seemed to be first to get interesting projects, and always weaseled her way out of the mundane tasks. However, if she did get put on a mundane task, she would ask our supervisor tons of ridiculously obvious questions, strictly to make it look like she was really interested.

Then one day, Jazmine called an "intern meeting." She said that the purpose of the meeting was to discuss everyone's goals, and what they'd like to do most during their time at the magazine. The meeting was awkward at best. Jazmine ran the meeting with a tone of "I'm the boss among us and I will report to our supervisor if you don't do as I say." None of the other interns had any desire to share their plans with each other. It turned out Jazmine wanted to make a file about each person's goals and ambitions, and hand it to our supervisor.

Important point: If the supervisor wanted to have such a meeting, she would have asked for it. Why would Jazmine do something that was not asked of her, and frankly, was intrusive? So Jazmine could get ahead, that's why. But none of us got it at the time, so we just went along with it.

Shortly after the meeting, people started getting odd assignments. For example, the smartest girl of the bunch, Alexa, was very quiet and sort of implied during our fabled intern meeting that she didn't care what she did. Later she made it clear that she only said that because she felt it was no one's business but her own and our supervisor's. But after the meeting, she was stuck with mail duty every day for the next three weeks. One day I overheard a conversation between Jazmine and one of our supervisors about how lazy and disinterested Alexa was.

Obviously, Jazmine was trying to make it seem as though she were the only trustworthy intern. And it worked for a while. People actually thought that Jazmine was trying to shoulder some of the burden for her poor fellow interns! Not so fast there, hotshot. The other interns and I talked about it, and we decided it was best to broach the topic with our other supervisors. When we did, they were not at all surprised and said that they had seen through her from the beginning, but other staffers actually bought her act. They also said that they weren't willing to make a big issue out of it, but that they would take the necessary steps to deal with Jazmine.

Things evened out after that, but the damage had been done.

WHEN YOU START TO IMMERSE YOURSELF IN YOUR NEW OFFICE'S SOCIAL REALM, IT'S ALWAYS BEST TO START WITH THE ONLY PEOPLE IN THE OFFICE WHO probably feel just as unimportant as you do: the other interns. Since forming relationships with coworkers is perhaps the hardest part of any job, practice your social etiquette on your equals first. It is most likely that the other interns are going to be your social group; they're around your age, and they're probably interested in many of the same things you are. However, they're also your biggest competitors!

When it comes to friendships and romances with fellow interns, it's best to always take it slow and really get a feel for someone before you think you've made a lifelong friend. Take it easy. Interns can be shadier than politicians if you catch them at the wrong moment.

First of all, every intern might have a different schedule, which leaves a lot of room for "he said, she said" crap. In other words, if you're not there on Fridays, don't put it past someone to say unflattering things about your work. Don't tell people personal things until you're totally comfortable with them. Stick to the standard discussions of education, partying, and sports until you're absolutely certain you're not having the wool pulled over your eyes.

WAYS TO TELL IF OTHER INTERNS ARE PLAYING YOU JUST TO TAKE YOU DOWN

- They're always smiling. . . . Real people frown.
- They talk a lot of shit about other interns to you, acting like you're the only one who's exempt. . . . When you're not around, you're the target!
- They're always "reporting" to your supervisor. . . . Even though they act like they're just doing their job, they're actually telling your supervisor how slow and lazy you truly are.
- They're constantly complimenting you. . . . Overcompensation, anyone?
- They say that you work harder than any of the other interns. . . . Translation: you're lazy, slow, incompetent, and you will be taken down.

When you're getting to know your fellow inmates, er, interns, treat everyone respectfully and don't bad-mouth anyone unless you want to sabotage your reputation by proving to your employer that you are an immature little kid who has no business being in an office. Remember, people still look at you as something just above a peon who occasionally makes a nice latte, which means that the moment you show yourself to be the least bit childlike or dramatic, you'll get pounced on without hesitation.

Keep the other interns on your side. You guys should feel like a team, even if there is a touch of healthy competition. In some ways professional athletes compete with their own teammates, but when it comes down to it, they're each other's biggest support system, which is exactly what a group of interns should be. Try to make things better as a group, while always distinguishing yourself, too. If you all share a common area, make sure that the last person to leave cleans it up, and leaves notes for the next day's interns in terms of any unfinished projects, so that everyone feels a real sense of camaraderie. However, while you're doing all of this wonderful team business, don't neglect yourself. You are still trying to stick out from the crowd, so follow the rules of going above and beyond at all times. Seek out your own assignments, and maybe enlist your fellow interns to help you, gently making sure everyone knows that it was your project to begin with.

You're probably wondering what this has to do with forming friendships outside of the office, right? Well, it all begins at work; how you parlay that relationship into something that stretches outside the office is the tricky part. The first step is lunch. When you go on your lunch break, don't go alone. Ask other interns if they want to go with you. You'll be a little freer to discuss non-work-related issues without all the constraints of a cubicle and the looming presence of supervisors.

Once you get to your lunch destination, start to engage your fellow interns in conversation that doesn't revolve around work. Ask about their social lives, their real aspirations, where they grew up, what they like to do on weekends. It takes most people an hour or so to decide whether they like someone and whether they want to establish any kind of non-work relationship. If you don't think there's any chemistry between you and another intern, that's fine. Don't worry about it, and don't let it affect your work. There's no room for sensitivity when you have a job to do, which is what complicates the social world of an office.

But remember this above all else: Don't make enemies. If it turns out that you went to lunch with someone who turned out to be nothing like you, they'll probably feel the same way, but you have to remain civil no matter what you really think of them. If your supervisor sees some kind of a rift between two interns, he'll just look at both of you as being immature, and thus unproductive, which is the opposite of what you're there to be. If you're causing the company any kind of unnecessary stress, there's a great chance you won't get a letter of recommendation out of them, and you may even be asked to leave. You have to prove that you don't need a babysitter before you prove how valuable you can be.

What if lunch goes well? In that case, start to treat your new buddy as exactly that: a real friend, albeit a new friend. Do whatever you would normally do to form a friendship. Ask the person to hang out on the weekend or after work. Invite him or her to things and try to accept invitations in return. Sound like too many rules for friendships? That's because you still work with these people, so you have to be on guard until the internship's finished, or at least until they've proven themselves to be true friends.

Start with a drink (those of you who are underage will be getting Shirley Temples, right?). It's always best to go one step at a time. The after-work drink is always a nice starting point. Try inviting a friend or two. It's best if you make plans with friends and then invite your fellow intern(s) to come along so as to prevent, or at least reduce, the amount of awkward silences a one-on-one drink will inevitably create. It's always safe to get others involved while getting to know someone; how you interact with a group is just as important as how you interact with someone on their own.

Once you've made a few friends, always remember that no matter how close you think you're becoming, you need to keep your guard up. If, for example, you're interning at a company for no other reason than to broaden your résumé, and you actually hate the work, you'd be better served by not telling your fellow interns, no matter how many blunts have been smoked or drinks have been had. Just say that you're really not sure what you want to get out of the experience, other than the experience itself. You never know. What if someone tragically screws something up in the office and there's a need for finger-pointing? Who's to say that your new friend won't point a finger at you and throw in the fact that you don't even really want to be working there? Or perhaps he or she mentions it to a friend when the boss is within earshot. Underneath it all, when it comes down to "me or him," people are generally going to pick themselves when a career or a reputation is on the line. You can't be totally paranoid, but you also can't be overly naive.

 Tip: Keep in mind that the people in the lower-level positions are going to be your best bet for making a few friends—aside from other interns—early on. If anyone will be able to sympathize with your plight, it will be these people.

If you're just a level or two below someone in a company and will one day likely be where they are, a working relationship that morphs into a friendship can be great. It's always nice to go to work and feel like you're among friends. However, in today's increasingly competitive job market, it's becoming harder and harder to find offices with a good vibe and a tightly knit staff, since everyone has to work really hard just to survive. Interning is no different. Even though it's challenging to mesh well, or at least appropriately with your fellow interns, it's more of a challenge to develop a solid relationship with real employees.

You should develop a comfortable working relationship with your supervisor before worrying about creating a friendship with him or her. First you have to show up on time every day and do everything you're asked to do. Only then will you even have a chance at earning enough respect from your supervisor for him or her to consider you adult enough to be a friend. It all starts in the office. Why would someone who you cause daily stress want to be your friend?

It's vital that you sort of sell yourself to, or at least be a little bit more vocal with, your supervisor than other employees. You know this from earlier chapters, but to reiterate, make sure your supervisor is your ally. Much like your advisor at school, your supervisor should be aware of your goals, your interests, your schedule, and the state of your life for as long as you are an intern. This doesn't mean that your supervisor should be your therapist, but he or she should be aware of what's going on with you.

Inform your supervisor of your exam schedule. If you have a week coming up when you know you're going to have a ton of work, or maybe even non-school-related engagements, like family or friends in town, make your supervisor aware of these things a few weeks in advance if you can. That way, if you have to switch your schedule around, or maybe even miss a day, your supervisor will know why and when in advance. Most companies are sympathetic to the fact that school takes precedence over everything, no matter what. However, if you're perpetually late or absent, don't expect much sympathy from anyone, regardless of your reasoning. Once you commit to an internship, you're being tested just as if you were a regular employee, which means no absences, excessive lateness, or lame excuses about your dog getting neutered on Tuesday at noon—you're gonna have to do better than that.

The key to the boss's heart lies in the file cabinet, the fax machine, the phone, and the professionalism you exude. Though the internship coordinator or your supervisor might be close to you in age, they're still real employees, with the responsibilities of real adults, and you're still their intern. In order for you to make the leap from little intern to soon-to-be successful young adult, you'll need to show that you are capable of the most important aspect of adulthood: working.

Assuming everything is going well—your boss frequently lets you know that you're doing a great job, you're comfortable in your office setting and thriving in your work—it may be time to befriend the boss! However, you need to be the reciprocator, not the one who starts the conversation. Wait until you think your boss wants to hang out with you before you try to hang out with your boss. Sometimes your boss will be totally cool and respectful to you inside the office, but not want anything to do with you once six o'clock rolls around (it's sorta like the girl in school who acts like your best friend in history class but won't talk to you in the courtyard—everyone loves that girl).

When your boss, or any employee for that matter, talks to you about anything other than the file cabinet cleaning project, make sure to take full advantage of the situation. However, don't be aggressive and over-bearing—it's annoying.

For example, if a few employees are sitting around discussing politics, and someone asks for your opinion, give it! Try not to worry about agreeing with everyone else—just try to participate in a truthful way. Employers look for young adults who can think on their own and have their own opinions, not kids who say what sounds good and constantly agree with everyone else. Anyone can do that, but few people can form their own opinions and stick to them at a young age.

This is business. While it's nice to make friends along the way, the most important part of your internship is getting substantial work experience under your belt. So if you don't make any new friends, don't take it personally, and don't waste time wondering why it hasn't happened.

If your supervisor invites you to a non-work-related event, you should go if you can. Depending on the size or nature of the event, it might be best to bring a friend. No, you're not trying to prove that you're not a friendless loser, just alleviating some of the pressure your boss might feel about inviting you to an event where you know no one and may also be younger than everyone else. Just make sure it's okay to bring someone before you do it.

Once you are in a nonwork setting with your supervisor, act as comfortable as you can be, even if you're actually fairly nervous (mind you, you may be nearing a mild heart attack, but try to get a grip). Most important, as always, is to be yourself. This isn't an interview. You're not trying to woo anyone. You don't have to be friends with your boss. Obviously you don't want to offend anyone, because whether or not you get along, you always have to keep that reference and contact on file, so try not to lose it right away.

Keep it cool. But not too-cool-for-school cool: Arrogance is annoying. Find the happy medium. Make sure your boss knows that you're really happy she asked you to hang out, but if you make her feel too important, she'll probably just get weirded out and never invite you out with her again. On the other hand, some people like nothing more than having their ego stroked, so figure out which kind of person your boss is and take it from there.

Conversationally, follow your supervisor's lead. Even though you're not in the office, you have to maintain a sense of professionalism when you're around anyone from work. As they loosen up, you can loosen up. At the end of the day, or night, you may realize that you really don't like them anyway, but that doesn't mean you can turn their invitations down—not if you ever want them to help you get a job.[5]

---

5. Ah, the shady world that is American business. It's so nice this time of year.

However loose things get, do not, under any circumstance, get too out of control on an intern-employee "first date." Even if your boss is doing shots off of someone else's back and dancing topless on the bar, just keep yourself under wraps . . . at least on your first excursion together.

HOW TO HANDLE WORK FUNCTIONS

 WHEN YOU'RE AT AN OFFICIAL WORK FUNCTION, YOU HAVE TO BE ON YOUR BEST BEHAVIOR FROM BEGINNING TO END. THIS IS CHALLENGING, BECAUSE some of the people you work for will probably be getting extremely drunk and may come down with a sudden case of verbal diarrhea. But you're not really seen as an adult, so the last thing you need is to risk getting too drunk and saying dumb things or behaving inappropriately. For some odd reason, when employees get out of control at a work function, it's often the basis of a few days of laughs. When an intern gets out of control at a work function, it's pretty much the beginning of the end.

Work functions are sort of like a second interview. Be humble, polite, and confident. Obviously, someone thought highly enough of you to give you an internship, so remember that you belong there. People will want to see that you can hold your own in adult conversations. You don't have to be a political genius or know anything about a home loan, but you'll need to be able to remain in a conversation even when you don't know what the hell anyone's talking about. Nodding is key. If you find yourself a little out of place or lost, just nod politely and ask questions if you're interested in the conversation (which you probably won't be). Don't be afraid to be naive about certain things—naïveté is still better than arrogance.

Interns often become a portal for employees' issues, so don't be surprised when you find yourself being told every last piece of intraoffice gossip there is. However, don't give an opinion; just nod and say things like, "really?" Obviously you'll have an opinion, but keep it to yourself when you're discussing other people in the office. In the morning hangovers start to wear off, employees are allied, and you're still just an intern.

Always be polite and mature. Address people in the same way you would in the office until someone says, "Loosen up kid, the day's over," at which point you can chill out a little with the contrived, mannered act. But still be respectful of all the employees. Consider the work function as an interview for a promotion. Apply the same basic rules; just think of it as trying to move up rather than merely get the gig.

Remember: You have to earn the right to act like a fool and be lazy when you please. It's probably best not to drink at all at work functions, but if you do, keep it to a one-drink maximum. You need to be clearheaded and ready to impress with any chance you get. Take advantage of your slobbering supervisor. Let her gush about her love life while you just listen like a real friend.

NETWORKING | CHAPTER 20

 PROBABLY THE SINGLE MOST VITAL COMPONENT OF THE SUCCESSFUL AMERICAN TODAY, NETWORKING IS A FULL-TIME JOB THAT CAN CATAPULT YOU above and beyond your competition, regardless of what field you're in. Essentially, a network is a group of people in the same—or a similar—industry, who you can turn to for favors, advice, and even jobs. The ultimate networking intern is someone who takes every card, every phone number, and every e-mail address of every person he or she meets and actually holds on to them. After all, you don't get a network, you build one.

Think about it: If you take fifty cards over the course of an internship, you'll have fifty connections that you can use for future internships or jobs. All you need is an e-mail address and the line "Hi, we met at the Wilson & Sanders holiday party last year. You said to get in touch with you if I ever wanted to intern for your company," and you're set. Networking is absolutely essential, because someone who doesn't mind networking at all times will make the most connections, and connections, as you know, are invaluable.

Networking is not reserved for work functions. Once you have an idea of the industry you'd like to work in, you need to have your ears open everywhere: at the store, at the club, at a bar, even in the damn library. When you hear of or meet someone who's in the same industry or could be of help to you, introduce yourself and try to form a connection.

When you're networking with people around your age, e-mail them the day after you meet and say, "Hey it was really nice to meet you last night. We should do it again sometime." This is where you have to learn to implement the social elements of interning, and eventually working. Your goal is to have as big a database as possible when you graduate from college, so you can contact everyone in that database in order to get a job, or get a lead on a job. As your career grows, so will your contacts.

Once you're out there in the real world, you can use the contacts that you made as an intern for real, important favors. You'd be shocked to learn how codependent seemingly unrelated industries are, so while you should focus on the industry you want to be a part of, take the plumber's card, too. How cool will it be when your entire office can't use the restroom and you, the helpless little intern, calls Joey the plumber, whom you met at some dive last week, and he/you save the day? Awesome!

What networking comes down to is using social adeptness to help your career. All the confidence you'll gain from your experiences interning will help you understand how to network and network well. When you're networking, you can draw on all your social skills and all your office etiquette, and you should have no trouble developing a long, worthy contact list. In the end, people will want *you* on *their* list too.

AND NOW, THE MOMENT YOU'VE ALL BEEN WAITING FOR: OFFICE HOOKUPS.

THIS IS RISKY BUSINESS. IT'S A LITTLE LESS stressful to hook up with another intern than with an actual employee, but dangerous nonetheless. First of all, considering most interns are somewhere between eighteen and twenty-two, mistakes will be made, and feelings will get hurt. While hooking up is a part of life, bringing that part of life into your office, especially an office where you're fairly unimportant, can be disastrous (or mind-blowingly exciting if you do it right!).

There are two kinds of office hookups: mistakes (usually one-time drunken affairs), and real office romances. The key is to keep it cool. In other words, nobody should know but the two people involved. Since you'll be dealing with all the things that come with a new relationship (lust, passion, long nights spent reading poetry, lying through your teeth, and ignoring all of your friends for a few months), you'll have to curb your enthusiasm while you're at the office. For example, if you're eating together every day and are perhaps mildly flirtatious, that's fine, but people will probably get it.

THINGS NOT TO DO WHEN DATING A FELLOW INTERN, ESPECIALLY IF YOU WANT TO LIE LOW

- **Fight in the office** While most healthy young couples argue, leave it on the street. If you can't work well together, you can't handle the relationship and the internship.
- **Make out in the lobby** Come on, guys, use your heads—save it for the stairwell!
- **Call each other cute little names in front of other employees** Could you be any more obvious, people?
- **Show up together, go home together** Even if you did spend the previous night together, leave a five-minute interval between each other's arrival and departure times.
- **Intentionally flirt with other employees to be passive-aggressive** Save the foolish games for after hours, please.
- **Propose during a morning meeting** This is just plain stupid.

An intern relationship is generally a huge taboo to most employers. Certainly some will be less rigid than others, but if you find yourself actually dating a fellow intern, be supercautious unless you know nobody will mind. That means that your supervisor has literally pulled you aside and said, "I know you and Megan are seeing each other, and that's fine, so long as it doesn't affect your work." The second an employer does start to see your productivity drop, the consequences could be drastic.

If you want to be taken seriously, the best thing to do, even if you have real feelings for someone you're interning alongside, is to simply keep it to yourselves. Tell each other how you feel once you leave the office.

What about meaningless little hookups? First of all, though this is not a book on relationships, it's safe to say that almost no hookups come without some kind of baggage, meaning, or bullshit. That's not to say that there aren't people who enjoy the random one-night stand, but hooking up with a fellow intern means you'll be seeing your fellow tongue-twister again very soon, whether you like it or not.

It's an old story. One person wants something more than the other person does, or someone gets hurt, or one person totally ignores the other person. While a "real" relationship isn't something you can control happening, you can control having a random hookup with potentially damaging consequences. The best advice: Keep it in your pants. Unless, before you even lock lips, you've discussed how you'll handle it after the fact.

That kinda takes the fun out of it, though, huh? Maybe, but if you have a morsel of self-control, you've got to try and be wise in these situations. This isn't a college classroom in which you've hooked up with half the room and nobody knows or cares who's doing what outside of class. This is work. This is a whole day spent with someone who you may or may not have wanted to hook up with in the first place.

Think about the consequences and the reality of such a situation. Random hookups always breed awkwardness; people get jealous, distant, spiteful, vulnerable, or too horny to control. You have to be supercareful if you're going to bring those elements into the workplace. Even though random hookups with fellow interns are not recommended, neither is hooking up with the ex-girlfriend you hate on a drunken night out with friends; sometimes things just happen. So prepare for the worst.

Okay, so you feel some sexual tension with one of the other interns, but you don't know if you should approach the situation with the standard return-of-the-flirts because of the repercussions. But you also think the person's really attractive, and you don't want to blow a chance at something. Time to grow up. Although one of the most enjoyable parts of hookups is the excitement that comes along with the not-having-to-think aspect, unfortunately, if you want to hook up with someone in the office, you're going to have to think before you act. Sad, isn't it?

Ask yourself:

- Do I really like this person?
- Is this really worth it?
- Is this person the type to go into the office and tell everybody?
- If people do find out, will I be let go?
- Can I just approach the person and discuss it beforehand?
- If I do that, will I even be attracted to the person by the time the conversation ends?
- Can I trust this person enough to know that they won't somehow use this against me later?

- Can I handle it?
- Can I afford another drink? This is really getting confusing!

See? You have to put so much effort into the initial thought that it's probably better to wait until the internship concludes. On the other hand, if things get out of control and end up happening anyway, here's a worst-case scenario list of how things will probably go down after the fact.

1. Someone lets the cat out of the bag.
2. The other party denies it.
3. The person who let the cat out of the bag is mortified because the other person won't admit to hooking up with them.
4. Other interns get involved.
5. The level of gossip reaches catastrophic proportions.
6. Going to your internship becomes more about dealing with the person you regretfully hooked up with than it does about the work itself.
7. Your supervisor gets tired of dealing with little kids.
8. Good riddance!

Now, was it really worth all this madness? It couldn't have been *that* good!

The only way two people can casually hook up while interning is if they're both extremely mature. That means being on the same page about what the hookup means before it happens. If two people decide that they really like each other, but think it would be wiser to put things on hold until after the internship, fine. If two people decide that they used, or are using, each other strictly for physical reasons, fine. But never let it affect your work.

"OFFICE FLINGS NEVER EQUAL DIAMOND RINGS" —MIKE

Okay, here's the scene: I'd been interning for an online magazine for about three months; it was the end of the summer, it was miserably hot. My internship coordinator walked into my cubicle and said, "Hey, Mike, this is Jennifer, our new intern. Jen, this is Mike. He's been here a while and will show you the ropes if you have any questions."

I stood to shake Jen's hand. She was an incredibly beautiful, thin, tall blonde. "Hi, Mike. Can we meet so I can ask you a few questions?" she said, with eyes that couldn't have meant anything but *I'd absolutely love to get to know you.*

"Um, sure," I said, a little thrown by her blatant aggressiveness. "Why don't we talk tomorrow?"

With a sly smile Jen replied, "I'll look forward to it, Mike."

When the day ended, Jennifer told me that she lived on Forty-third Street and Eighth Avenue, and somehow already knew that I lived on Fifty-first and Seventh. She asked if she could walk home with me. So we began walking from our office, talking along the way about love and relationships. We began to approach Forty-third

Street as we walked up Broadway, so I said, "I guess you're going that way, so I'll see you next week."

"Oh, no," she said, "I'm going to a friend's on Fifty-second Street, so I'll walk with you."

I thought nothing of it. But while crossing Forty-fourth Street, she suddenly told me that she hadn't had sex in two years and that wouldn't be changing any time soon—with a man, that is. Then, three minutes later, standing on the corner of Forty-sixth Street waiting for the light, she seemed to be in a daze. I turned and asked her what was on her mind. One word came out of her mouth: "You," she said, looking me dead in the eye.

I slowly picked my jaw up off the filth-ridden sidewalk and said, "Um, okay. I, um, yeah . . ."

Looking back, I never should have even let this chick into my apartment. But hormones are a killer, aren't they? The next few hours will have to be saved for a filthier book, but we crossed some lines that could not be erased, and we were still fellow interns.

I didn't see her until two days later, at which point she essentially acted not only as if nothing had happened, but as if she hated me. By then, I saw the shitstorm forming quickly out of the empty office cubicles and engulfing me into a potentially very bad situation. So I told both of my bosses exactly what was going on so that if Jennifer attempted anything even remotely shady, I would already be a step ahead of her. Jennifer and I proceeded to awkwardly ignore each other for a week or so.

Meanwhile, I had been really interested in an old friend for years, and despite this little escapade, I planned on courting her that same weekend.

Saturday came, and I did in fact profess my feelings for the girl I truly liked and she felt the same way. We were officially dating by the next week, so anything more with Jennifer was absolutely out of the question. My friends around the office were aware of the situation and began speaking openly in front of Jennifer about my new girlfriend. Late on a Tuesday afternoon, after all the interns were setting up for an event, Jen somehow managed to get me alone on the way home.

When we left, Jen said she'd like to walk with me for a while because she felt bad about how she had acted and wanted to be friends. I agreed, and we began walking. As we approached Thirty-ninth Street and Seventh Avenue, Jennifer, after acting completely normal for the last half hour, grabbed me and said, "Just take me upstairs and make out with me one last time." I explained to her that I couldn't—I was seeing someone. Jennifer didn't take this well at all. She screamed, "Oh, God! You never loved me! I knew it!"

I began walking away. She caught up with me and said quietly, "Just once more, please, please, please, or I'll have you fired. I swear."

After peeling her off of me I made a quick sprint to my apartment and immediately called my boss.

The next few day, when Jennifer realized she wasn't going to get me, she had a complete breakdown while running an errand. She called the office to say she fainted, and no one saw her again. She called me once or twice after that, but, needless to say, I had learned my lesson.

PART V | THE BEGINNING OF THE END

THE FINAL WEEKS OF AN INTERNSHIP ARE NOT A TIME TO LET YOUR GUARD DOWN, BUT RATHER A TIME TO WORK EXTRA HARD AND TAKE INVENTORY.

Ask yourself, above all, if you think you might want to work for this company after you graduate. If so, take this advice:

- Show up on time, and never miss a day, especially at the end.
- Work even harder than you have been all along.
- Meet with your supervisor/coordinator.
- Find out in which areas you could improve.
- Find out in which areas you were perfectly strong.
- Attempt to improve any weak points during your final days.
- Ask any questions you might have.
- Discuss the future.
- Obtain a reference, preferably in writing.
- Leave on a good note, even if you're completely full of it!

What not to do:

- Come in hungover each and every day.
- Profess your love for your boss.
- Profess your hatred for Jack in HR.
- Do as little as possible.
- Smoke in the stairwell.
- Set some small field mice free in the office, sending the entire staff into a frenzy, eventually causing the office to be evacuated.
- Do as little as humanly possible when you do actually make it to the freakin' office.

FROM THE INTERN FILES OF THE INTERNSHIP COORDINATOR

For students who intern in spring of their senior year, turning an internship into a job often comes down to whether there is a job opening at the time you complete the internship. Make a good impression and a company will either try to find a position for you, help you find a job elsewhere, or keep you in mind if something opens up at a later date. During my tenure, we have hired seven former interns. Being in the right place at the right time is really the key to landing a job after your internship is over.

Now that you know what to do about your performance, here's what to do about your feelings. You've spent a lot of time focusing on the present to this point, but as the internship winds down, you also need to focus a bit on the future, while still being the best intern you can be. A few weeks before your internship is scheduled to end, take notice of non-intern-related issues:

- Are the employees generally happy? If you have any friends who are paid employees, don't be afraid to politely ask them if their salaries are commensurate with the industry standards.
- Is there room for movement within the company, or is the assistant in his or her fifteenth year, unable to get a better position even though he or she is fully qualified?

What's great about taking a little extra time to look at your internship before it's complete is that you can ask to try something you really wanted to do. Whether you wanted to use the super-mega-high-tech fax machine or you wanted to write for the publication where you are an intern, approach your supervisor and say, "You know, I was never really able to use the fifth-floor fax. Do you think I could give it a shot before I leave?"[6] The end of an internship is a time when doors will sometimes fly open, rather than slam in your face.

If you take a close look at your time at the company and realize that you have been late a few too many times, or that you haven't put as much effort into a certain area as you would have liked, you still have time to make up for it. Show up five minutes early every single day for the rest of

6. Hopefully, you'll want to do more than use the fifth floor fax.

the month; put extra care into any area you feel you've neglected. Things can change. By focusing on improving your weaknesses (and we've all got them), you might just change someone's mind about you. Your image is not set in stone. In fact, some employers will notice and be impressed with the fact that you are able to identify areas where you are lacking and to improve on them without being told to do so. And your supervisor will be watching you especially closely. The last thing supervisors want to see is interns slacking off because they're almost done. This is just the beginning. If you treat the situation otherwise, rest assured that your company will think that you have no interest in working for them, and they'll have no interest in hiring you or writing you a reference.

You don't lose anything by ending on a high note, working hard, and keeping the door unlocked behind you as you leave. And you may gain a strong reference and the potential to stay in contact with other employees. Why do you want to stay in contact with employees if you hated your internship and don't care for the industry? Because when it comes to your career, you should never burn a bridge. As long as you don't despise your supervisor or the company, and they still think highly enough of you, don't worry about the internship itself, think of the future. Who says that the one employee you actually got along with and who seemed to see your potential won't be working for the company of your dreams by the time you graduate? Wouldn't it be nice to have that person say, "Oh yeah, I remember Jim. He seemed like a bright kid even when he was in college and was still interning," rather than, "Oh yeah, Jim. He didn't even take the time to have an exit interview when he interned at my last company. I wouldn't advise hiring him." And no matter how different the industry that you want to work in is from the one you interned in, you'll always need a good reference.

People tend to remember the last thing you did as an intern. If you slacked off but made up for it in the end, employers will at least recognize that you tried, even if was too little, too late. If you were unhappy and decided not to have an exit interview and showed up late your last five days, it won't soon be forgotten.

AS YOUR INTERNSHIP STARTS TO WIND DOWN, YOU HAVE TO START THINKING ABOUT YOUR NEXT MOVE. IF YOU'RE A SENIOR, YOU'LL BE DRIVING yourself up the wall trying to figure out what to do with your life. If you've got more schooling left, maybe you're just thinking about your next internship. Either way, the first order of business as your internship nears its end is to evaluate yourself and your experience as an intern.

- Did you find your internship met the expectations you had when you began?
- Did your performance meet your own goals and expectations?
- What did you get out of the experience?
- Would you consider working at this company after you've completed college?

If you absolutely hated your experience, keep that to yourself. In the last few weeks of your internship, you're basically on a full-time exit interview. Your school will likely have you evaluate your experience and performance in writing. Your internship supervisor at work will be evaluating you and sending your advisor at school a review of your performance, and perhaps a grade to boot. Also, you'll want to have a formal exit interview, which entails sitting down with your supervisor, and maybe with a human resources specialist, and discussing your experience and what you might want to do next. The exit interview is sort of an evaluation of your experience as an intern and the company's role as an employer. However, some companies don't actually have formal exit interviews, so while you'll need to know what to do in a formal setting, remember that in many ways your presence alone will determine how you're remembered.

If you're unsure about how you performed or how you think the company viewed your performance, approach your supervisor or coordinator about a month before the internship concludes and simply say, "I was hoping we'd get a chance to meet before the internship ends so we can go over my performance and discuss any future possibilities."

Once you've scheduled your exit interview, you'll have to begin to make the toughest evaluation of all: your own.

Start by asking yourself some key questions:

- Did I work as hard as I possibly could?
- What could I have done better?
- Did I enjoy this industry?
- Did this company turn out to be as phenomenal as I had expected?
- What did I learn?

- What was most beneficial to me, and what could I have done without?
- Can I do anything in the last month to help myself, or is there anything I haven't done that I'd like to?

If you're feeling like you were shortchanged in terms of being given any final opportunity to review things with your supervisor, focus more on your self-evaluation; most likely you have an even better understanding about how you performed than your supervisor.

In one sense, interning is all about impressing employers and proving yourself. In another sense, however, internships, much like college, are all about learning about yourself and seeing what it is you enjoy, where you might want to take your career, and what you'll want to avoid altogether.

Hopefully you're preparing for a formal exit interview. If the opportunity hasn't been offered to you, ask for it. There are several key factors that are going to play into how honest your supervisor is going to be with you. If you formed a strong working relationship with him or her, were generally on time, worked as hard as you possibly could, and never came to work wasted and passed out on your desk, you've got a good shot.

But no matter what, there's no reason why you shouldn't have a final conversation, formal or informal, with your supervisor in which you hear how you performed in every area of your internship, where your strengths were, and what your weaknesses were. Essentially, you're asking them if they would hire you if given the chance, and if not, why not.

This is merely another lap on the test drive, for both the intern and the employer. Although it's important that you ask questions throughout your internship, the end is the time where you really want to learn as much as you can about how you did, what you could have done better, and how your attitude was perceived—everything you worked so hard at is now culminating. And the experience is even more worthwhile if you're able to find out exactly what your company's employees thought about how you handled yourself.

In the exit interview itself, your goals are to:

1. Get as much information on your own performance as you can
2. Discuss the possibility of returning as a full-time employee (if you're interested in that)
3. Leave on a positive note

Assuming you do get the chance to sit down with your supervisor in a formal setting, here's what to do and what to say.

When you sit down, say, "First of all, I really wanted to thank you for the opportunity to have interned here."

Always be grateful before you get into the details. The criteria for your meeting should be the same as the self-evaluation. You want to find out from your supervisor:

• Did I meet your expectations, and if not, why not?
• What could I have done better?
• What were my strongest areas?
• What advice can you give me based on my performance here?

What happens in every exit interview will be different, based on the nature of the company and your relationship with your supervisor, but try to cover those bases, no matter how much you digress during the meeting itself. And be prepared. Since you're discussing the future, tell them your graduation date, make sure they have all your contact information, and try to make sure that they're aware of your accomplishments.

Even if you don't impress anyone, or if you kinda flew under the radar and never discussed your performance with anyone, focus on your self-evaluation.

- What could you have done to make yourself more visible?
- Did you, in your own mind, work to your utmost capacity (and if not, why not)?
- Was the company a bad fit for you?

These are the questions that you can ask yourself and discuss with your advisor at school after the fact. You may not have gained much, but really, you've lost nothing at all. No internship is a waste of time. Worst-case scenario, it wasn't a step in the right direction, but it's still a good line on your résumé.

WHAT IF YOU HATED IT? | CHAPTER 24

 SO WHAT IF, LIKE MANY INTERNS, YOU LEAVE YOUR EXPERIENCE NOT REALLY KNOWING HOW YOU FELT ABOUT IT, AND STILL TOTALLY UNSURE OF WHAT you want to do? LIE! Tell your supervisor that you loved every moment of it and you'd give a limb to work for the company down the road. (Just kidding, what if you actually got hired? Yikes!) In reality, all you have to do is be honest about your experience during your exit interview. Say that you are grateful for the experience, and that you enjoyed yourself and learned a lot. However, you're not sure the industry is right for you. Be diplomatic. Remember: Keep those doors swinging!

If you hated every waking moment of your internship: *Do not tell anyone at the company!* If you didn't hate it enough to quit, have a nervous breakdown, or injure anyone at the company, you can probably stand to have a nice, pleasant, albeit enormously disingenuous exit interview. Just be appreciative, but feel free to speak your mind, unless you think it'll be counterproductive. Here are some ways to politely address the fact that you were unhappy with your internship:

- I felt like I was never really given the chance to show what I can do. If I had been, I feel I could have showed you guys that I'm capable of much more.
- Since my days were so scattered, I was never really given enough consistent work to get in a groove.
- My school schedule conflicted with my work schedule to the point where I was always too rushed or stressed out to perform to the best of my ability.
- I was nervous. I had no office experience before now and am glad I got this internship under my belt, even though I know I could have done better.

Do you notice the common thread here? You suggested that you could have been given more responsibility, but you never pointed a finger anywhere but at yourself. Even if you feel you weren't given a fair shake, make sure you don't whine about it—nobody likes a whiner. And don't make excuses—give reasons. If you really felt like you weren't there enough, or your schooling conflicted with your schedule to the point that you were perpetually rushed or stressed out, don't imply that it was anyone's fault but your own.

If you learn anything while you intern, it should be that you're the only person responsible for yourself and your life. *You* could have changed your schedule. *You* could have told someone sooner. If you do give excuses, not only will your supervisor have responses for each and every one, but he or she will think that you're incapable of taking charge of your own life and that you'd rather complain than just do.

Lastly, if you had a personal problem with an employee or a fellow intern; if you found out that the president of the company took money from a nefarious character; or if you just thought everyone was totally incompetent—it's probably better that you don't share that information with anyone but your friends and your advisor.

If you actually make it through an internship without getting fired or rubbing people the wrong way, even if you hated it and learned nothing except that you never want to have anything to do with this company again, you still might have gained some contacts you can call for jobs later. In business, it's all business, even as an intern.

WHETHER OR NOT YOU'RE GRADUATING, MOST OF YOU WILL WANT TO OBTAIN A LETTER OF REFERENCE, REGARDLESS OF HOW YOU ACTUALLY FELT about your internship. If you're not offered one, asking is perfectly acceptable—as long as you do it appropriately. If you ask, and your supervisor politely declines, there's your evaluation in a nutshell; don't sweat it, just work ten times harder at your next internship. Or believe him when he says the company has a policy of not providing references. Sometimes that's actually true.

If your evaluation was poor, save yourself the embarrassment and don't ask for a reference. If the company didn't think you were strong as an intern, why would they want to sign a piece of paper that outlines your strengths? Don't bother asking.

If your evaluation was actually strong, you're on solid ground. If you're lucky enough to have a written reference offered to you, graciously accept. However, it's more likely you'll have to ask, which shouldn't be very difficult or pressure-filled if you know you've done a good job. Either at the end of a formal exit interview, or really anytime during the last few weeks, simply approach your supervisor in person or by e-mail and say, "I wanted to ask if it would be possible to get a written reference. Not only did I enjoy my time working at your company, but I also know how highly respected the company is and would love to be able to show any future employers that I performed well as an intern here."

In the letter of recommendation, your employer should speak on all of your strengths, possibly highlight a few key examples of how exactly those strengths manifested themselves, and then conclude the letter by saying something like, "I would strongly suggest considering Tom for employment at your company. If you have any questions, call me at 1-(800)-INTERNS, and I'd be happy to discuss Tom in further detail."

Some employers may say that you can use them as a reference, but they won't be willing to write formal letters. While an available reference is nice, and will become essential when you enter the job market, a written document on company letterhead, signed by an employee with a nice title, is a beautiful thing.

Hint: Very few interns apply by sending a résumé, cover letter, and written references. If you have one or more references, always include them in your application. Wouldn't you rather hire someone who comes with references, rather than having to make five phone calls on your own time?

If you were well liked and worked hard, people will actually *want* to attach themselves to you, and they will be more than happy to be the one who recommends the outstanding employee. You've gone from a peon to a hot commodity in mere months!

WITH A FEW PHENOMENAL INTERNSHIPS UNDER YOUR BELT, YOU'RE A HOT COMMODITY. IN MANY CASES, COMPANIES VALUE A YOUNG, FRESH ATTITUDE as much as they do experience. With solid internships on your résumé, you've got both. You're young, but you're not inexperienced. You're experienced, but you're not graying, either. So even if the supervisor from your first internship can't help you himself, he might have a friend at another company who's looking for interns, and he'll send you their way.

Even if you're not graduating for two years, you still need to think of every internship as a building block for the future. If you absolutely loved your internship, the most important part of your final days as a peon is letting the company know how you feel and leaving an impression strong enough to last for a couple of years. If you liked your internship, but aren't sure if you'd want to come back as a real employee, that still doesn't mean that the company can't be of help to you down the road. If you absolutely loathed every minute of the experience, you know that you still have to leave on a good note, right?

If you think that the company for which you've just interned is a place that you could see yourself working down the road, keep that bridge sturdy and you might get more than a recommendation. Keep the company abreast with your life. Constantly update them on where else you're interning and any projects you might be working on. However, in order to do this, you need to have a strong enough relationship with at least one person there that you can call to discuss these things with, which is why making friends—or at least work-related allies—is so important; your character is judged just as closely as your work. If you think you might want to work for that company down the road, don't end the relationship once your internship is over. Stay in contact with a person or two at the company in the years to come. This doesn't mean that you should call them every time you successfully avoid peeing on the seat, but when you get or conclude other internships or if you're deciding between two offers, don't hesitate to call your old bosses and tell them about it, or ask for help.

Employers love dedication—perhaps more than good work. If you actually maintain a strong relationship with a company for which you've interned, they'll know that you are, above all, a driven, detail-oriented, dedicated machine of an ex-intern. When the time comes for you to enter the job market, they're going to want you just as much as you want them.

INTERNSHIP TO JOB

If you're graduating, or perhaps looking for part-time employment, make sure your internship supervisor and the powers that be are aware of this so that they can keep you in mind as much as you've kept them in mind. If there is in fact a job opening as your internship is ending, and they want to hire you, they'll probably broach that issue with you directly—but don't be afraid to bring it up!

If there is an opening, and you're not hired, don't let that get you down. It doesn't mean you weren't an exceptional intern; there was probably just someone more qualified than you were. While it does sometimes happen, getting hired immediately after an internship is not something to expect. It's a bit of a risk to intern during your last semester of college in hopes that the company will hire you just because you're there and graduating, and it's also not wise to bank on any former internships to come through with jobs immediately. While you should always go back and ask for help, no one is required to hire you just because you were a stellar intern.

"I'VE BEEN WAITING FOR THIS OPPORTUNITY FOREVER!"
—LAURA

While attending college here in Seattle, I got pretty heavy into a scene I swore I'd avoid at all costs: the Northwest indie rock scene. Growing up in Florida, I was more into Latin-influenced music and techno—you know, things you can actually dance to.

Anyway, I went up to a small school in Seattle. So I figured, "What the hell. I've always loved music, let me try to get involved around here." I had a friend who was a senior and said that she had interned for this really great little music studio that was now helping her look for a job. She explained to me how the internship program worked and what I had to do, and she gave me some helpful advice on working and going to school while still occasionally managing to get some sleep.

The small company thing sounded nice, but I wanted to do something bigger—something more important. However, I couldn't see how I would be able to do that with no experience behind me. So I referenced my friend's name and my internship director's advice, and began to seek out gigs at local record companies. There was only one place I truly wanted to be, but that particular company was seemingly impossible to get to. So I bit the bullet.

What I did was intern for two separate companies, one less important than the other, and learned as much as I could. The day I graduated college, I got a call on my cell phone from a mysterious number. When I picked up, the voice sounded vaguely familiar. Who do you think it was?

If you said my friend who was a senior when I was first intern-ing, you guessed right. This friend, whom I'd basically lost touch with, was now in a fairly powerful position at the music group for which I initially wanted to work—her dingy little internship at her dingy little company had gotten her the gig—and now she asked if I was looking for work. Obviously, I jumped at the chance. After I sent her my résumé and her bosses reviewed it, she called me in for an interview and I was, in the end, hired.

The man who interviewed me said that while I was not the most experienced candidate for the just-above-entry-level position, I had three things going for me. First, I was a friend of one of his favorite employees. And I had internship experience at two small, but respectable, record companies. But above all, I was "well liked," as he put it. Turns out my hard work as an intern hadn't gone unnoticed. When he called the two record companies I had interned for, he was given such impressive reviews that he immediately hired me.

**YOU KNOW HOW TO FIND THESE ELUSIVE INTERN-
SHIPS. YOU KNOW HOW TO *GET* THESE MYSTERIOUS
WONDERMENTS. YOU KNOW WHAT TO DO WHEN**
you get there, and you even know what to do when you leave. You also
know how to be the world's greatest intern—so what's your excuse? You
have none! So go take charge!

College is all about maturing while staying as young and as foolish
as possible, but you'll have to grow up sometime. Internships are very
similar; you mature in so many ways, but you're also given chances you
won't be given once you're a working adult. So while you work, you also
learn, and you are allowed a mulligan or two that can be blamed on inex-
perience and youthful zest. Once you enter the workforce, you can kiss
those second chances good-bye, so appreciate your role as a peon while
you still can.

The last piece of advice *The Intern Files* can give current and future
interns is to read this book again, take notes along the way (seriously),
and tell all your friends to read the book too. If you pay close enough

attention to the advice given; if you listen to your advisors, your supervisors, and your peers; then you'll be ready to hit the ground running when you—gasp—graduate from college.

The job market is getting more competitive every day, and there are no signs of this trend changing any time soon. That means that internships are growing in value by the moment too, which means that you'll have to work that much harder, and be that much more experienced, than the next person.

Above all, you should look at internships as small blessings that don't come along too often. They may just be the keys to a door that you didn't even know existed. Although you do have to work hard, and you do have to be on top of your game at all times, your hard work will pay off. When you graduate, you'll have so many experiences to draw on that you'll radiate confidence. You'll have done so many things already that while non-former peons are still trying to figure out which industry they might want to think about, you'll have a strong sense of what you want to do with the beginning of your career.

Even if you only learned that you don't want to be a part of the American workforce—that you'd rather be an artist or live in another country—wouldn't you rather have learned that through interning as opposed to learning it on the job?

There's no way to go wrong by interning while you're in college. Even when you feel like you lost something or you were totally taken advantage of, you'll know how to troubleshoot the situation in the future. Even if you got let go from an internship, at least it wasn't a "real job" that could have left you blacklisted from an entire industry. Maybe you found your calling, or maybe you found that you just don't have a calling quite yet. That's still something, isn't it?

Feelin' ready to make coffee yet? You psyched to make copies? Pumped to print? Excited about answering phones? Well, you should be, because you might just answer a call that becomes the door to your future! Good luck! (And don't forget my 5 percent!)

 "HARD WORK PAYS OFF" —ALLEGRA

During the last semester of my senior year in college, I interned at a small marketing group in New York City for no credit and no pay whatsoever. I was unable to receive credit because I had used up the maximum amount of credits you were allowed to get from the intern program (apparently, schools say you have to go to class, too), and this company never paid its interns, so I elected to do the internship anyway with my near future in mind. No dough, no credits—nada—just an internship and a dream.

I was finishing school, summer was coming up, and even though I just wanted to relax and think about what I would do with my life after momentarily basking in the glory of a college degree, I wasn't from New York, and I really wanted to stay after I graduated. That meant I'd have to do a little more than the next guy or gal if I wanted to remain in the city I'd grown to love.

So I took the internship and worked while I was in school and throughout the summer. My social life was lacking, my grades were a little lower than my personal standards, but I did what I had to do. I had class all day Monday and Wednesday, and went to my internship on Tuesdays, Thursdays, and Fridays. However, the company did a lot of work with musicians, which meant they also did a lot of work at music events, which called for a lot of late-night work. I could have opted not to work at or attend any of these events, but I knew that in order to get hired, I would have to prove that I was willing to go above and beyond. I worked from May through August nearly every day and never saw a dime—but I knew it was coming.

You can probably guess where this story is going—yep, I got hired at the end of the summer. There was no guarantee. I could have been jobless after I worked for absolutely nothing, but I worked harder than anyone else at the company and it showed. I arrived earlier and stayed later than the paid employees. I stayed at events (to represent the company, of course) until four o'clock in the morning, and then went to class at eight, and I never let my employer hear me complain about it, but I know that she knew it was hard. When I was in the office, I took on as much work as any employee at the twelve-person firm, and that didn't go unnoticed either.

There are different tactics when it comes to parlaying an internship into a real job. Mine was simple: I told my employer when I took the internship that I needed a job at summer's end, whether with them or with someone else. The point is that I informed them of my situation early enough so that I was prepared when the summer concluded. I was very fortunate to have a job offer by mid-August, without ever having to sit down and ask for a job.

But I don't feel lucky. I feel deserving to have gotten a job that dozens were vying for. I worked my ass off and never said a word about it—except for bitching to my friends, that is. Had I opted to be lazy and not intern because I wasn't getting anything tangible out of it, like credit or money, I don't know if I would have been able to live where I wanted to live, or if I even would have gotten a job so soon after graduation. But let's not get carried away—I'm an assistant, not a VP. I'm still paying my dues, but interning taught me how to suck it up and work through any extra pressure, knowing that there is always a payoff for people who actually commit to something, even in corporate America! So even if you're feeling beaten down by the hard work you're putting in, or if you're feeling like you may never be appreciated, give everything your best shot. Interning is like life: you don't always get something tangible in return for what you do, but it usually pays off in the end.

 "ASKING THE RIGHT QUESTIONS" —ERIN

While I was in college, I was able to intern for only one semester at a nonprofit arts foundation. However, I sit here today, four years later, at the same desk that I used when I interned. Back when I was interviewing for internships, my advisor at school told me that when interviewing, I should ask each potential employer a direct question: What is the percentage of interns who end up getting hired on a full-time or freelance basis?

I was a junior at the time, so although I saw her point, I wondered if that was really the best criteria to base my internship selection on. My advisor told me that it was in my best interest to intern for a company that is prone to hiring former interns. My school allowed only one internship, and my advisor said it wouldn't be easy to get a job in such a competitive field.

I have to admit, I thought this woman was crazy. I was attending a top art school, getting a degree in art history, and my grades were incredibly strong. I knew art. I loved art. But my advisor asked, "Since you don't plan on creating it, do you know how to *work* with art?" No, I didn't.

"But doesn't nonprofit mean that you're not really making money anyway?" I asked.

With a paralyzing smirk, my advisor simply said, "You have a lot to learn."

I left that meeting and began to research the term "nonprofit" and make a list of organizations in Chicago, where I was from, and where I planned to return for my summer internship. My list ended up totaling seven, and I asked each potential site through phone interviews (I was at school in Connecticut) how many of their current employees were former interns. The answers ranged from none to 100 percent. The company that had all former interns was a small nonprofit organization run by a husband and wife who started the company on their own and initially had only a single "employee"— a Northwestern business student who interned for them and did their books, and made about forty bucks a week. That girl became the company's backbone, handling all monetary issues as well as all of their PR.

From that point on, said my interviewer, every intern had been hired as the company grew, and thus each had a vital role. The company had a total of eleven employees, all of whom had been interns. He said that the founders were set on having a family-oriented business whose employees were sort of homegrown. "You know, like a minor league ball player making it to the bigs and retiring with that same club twenty years later," he said. I was being interviewed by an art person making baseball analogies and telling me how much he loved his job—I needed to work for them!

So I took the internship, had a great summer, learned literally as much as any one person could in three months, and was assured that when I graduated, there would be a job for me if I wanted it, assuming that the company was "still in existence." And they were true to their word. Moments after I woke up the day after graduation, still groggy from graduation-night debauchery, I called up Jerry, one of my former supervisors. I told him that I'd graduated and that I'd love to come back and work for them. He said they'd need two weeks or so, and lo and behold, two weeks later Jerry called and said they had created an entry-level position for me and that I could start as soon as I was ready.

I took the job and am still here and moving up on the food chain. But I attribute my good fortune to that one question: "What percentage of your employees are former interns?" It was the best question I have ever asked anyone in my life. Since everyone's situation, dreams, and goals are so specific, it's important that college kids address those issues while they're in school. As a twenty-year-old student, I needed my advisor to make me ask that question. Her vision was one rooted in experience and driven toward the future—my future—a future that has now arrived, thanks to my advisor's foresight.

"THE INTERN FILES IS BORN" —JAMIE

Every so often, we hear stories that are borderline miraculous, ridden with hard work, a touch of fate, and perhaps some luck, too. I have one of my own. From late August 2004 until mid-December 2004, I was interning for a now canceled late-night talk show on a major network while finishing my alleged last semester of college. I had a ton of work to do at school, my internship necessitated a commute from New York City to nearby New Jersey (which was practically another time zone with rush hour traffic), and the show was, shall we say, fledgling at best.

Nonetheless, I had four remaining credits that could be used for an internship, and I figured I'd try my hand in the TV industry. I hoped that it would materialize into a job after college. The internship was a struggle. Interns weren't really given any legitimate responsibility— outside of handling B-, C-, and D-list guests as they trickled onto the show, and doing immense amounts of research. I did, however, once carry our host in nothing but his boxers from his office down the hall for a segment, which was a pretty vital/disgusting moment in my career.

In retrospect, I became so disillusioned with the TV industry (we had seen three executive producers get hired and fired in a matter of months), and with the internship itself, that I really just did what I was asked and didn't go above and beyond. There wasn't really any room for that, since the staff was trying to save the show and their jobs. Then one day, the first in a chain of *seemingly* hollow moments occurred.

The show had a cohost who wasn't getting much airtime and wasn't really able to contribute to the program as much as he would have liked. So one day after a double taping we got to talking, and I found out that while we were miles apart in terms of our careers, we had a lot in common: We both felt unappreciated, we both felt like we wanted to do more but were stifled, we both felt useless, and we both felt (despite his hefty salary and my nonexistent pay) we were wasting our time and we wanted out, yet we were both worried about what we would do, with the inevitability of the show's cancellation looming.

At the end of the conversation, kind of in jest, he said, "Ya know, you have so many experiences as an intern, both good and bad, you oughta write a damn book about it so that kids don't make some of the same mistakes that you made. What could make more sense for someone who wants to be a writer than writing about part of what they've just been through in the last few years, right?"

And then it all clicked. Having always wanted to be a writer, and wholeheartedly believing that writers are at their best when they write what they know, what did I know better than internships? I mean, nearly a quarter of my college credits were from interning, and I had enough advice/material to go on for years. So after our conversation, I went home to my ridiculously overpriced cubicle of an apartment in Manhattan and began penning *The Intern Mantra*. By about three a.m. I had something in front of me that was both valuable and worthwhile . . . and I knew it. It was a ranting piece of critical shit at that moment, but I knew that people, college kids particularly, could relate to the humor, necessity, and sheer commonality of the experience of interning. Who hadn't worked a shitty job or two? Who hadn't interned and possibly been taken advantage of? How many people my age did I know who were constantly talking about the daily ins and outs of their internships?

But there was a problem: I was no success story. I was working for a show where I didn't think my hard work was noticed, as limited as it was, and I hadn't tried to contact any of my old supervisors yet, so who was I to talk? Then it happened. The "mantra" became a tangible idea with an interested publisher and has become what you are about to finish reading. But here's the twist: On December 15, 2004, I found out that I'd gotten this book deal, and the show I was interning for was canceled around the same time. I, of course, agreed to write the book, and that became my job right out of college. About a month later, I went to a party for my internship coordinator from the show, and one of the writers from the show—we'll call him Arnold—asked me how the book was going.

"Great," I said. "It's a huge opportunity."

"Good thing the show got canceled then, huh?" Arnold said, laughing.

"What does that have to do with anything?" I asked.

"Wait, you didn't know?"

"What the hell are you talking about, man?" I asked, my curiosity growing.

"The morning the show got canceled we had a meeting about creating a job for you," Arnold said with a smirk.

"What?" I really was shocked. I thought most of the people at the show didn't know I existed. "But I never even got to do anything worth a shit. What would my job have been?"

"I don't know," Arnold began. "I just know that we were trying to figure out a way to bring you onto the show because the people who mattered noticed every last minute of good work you did, and understood your disillusionment with the way things were going. Anyway, we got canceled that same day, so the issue of your employment was obviously moot, but I just wanted you to know that you were appreciated and we really would have liked to hire you."

First, it was nice to know that the people I admired respected me, particularly when I thought just the opposite was true. But more importantly, I couldn't have been more thankful to the network for canceling the show. I probably would have taken the job, had it been offered to me, and put this book on hold. It sounds selfish because people did lose their jobs, but they all bounced back, and for me, the internship I thought was useless actually ended up being the beginning of this book.

So I may be lucky enough to say that I am a true intern success story. We all have a niche somewhere. Outside of a few stellar semesters, school was not mine. I always figured that interning would be the start of my road to wherever the hell I'm going, and I was right; it's just that I thought the outcome would be more like getting a PA gig on a low-rated talk show.

Not only am I proud to share this sort of "it could happen to you" story, but I'm also proud to reflect on and pass on this advice: No matter what your feelings are about your internship, forget them, and do your damn work no matter what. I was frighteningly close to leaving my last internship early because I was being an immature shithead and thinking, "I just can't take it anymore," though by staying, I find myself, a year later, in the fortunate position of penning *The Intern Files*. I also left the show with great contacts and insight into the TV industry.

The point is, my story could be anyone's. My career is headed in a different direction now, but what if there were no book? I most definitely would have bothered every last employee from all of my internships until I had a job. In fact, I have already contacted a few of them, and they've all been happy to put their stamp of approval on my résumé and help me look for jobs.

Thank you to the show that got canceled, particularly to the show's cohost and to the network that canceled it. Without the bizarre experience of working for your show, I would never have been able to write this book.

You never know what can come of an early morning commute and a few trips to the coffeemaker.

SOME INTERNSHIPS BY REGION

MIDDLE ATLANTIC

ABC News *Nightline*

Accuracy in Media

Alliance for Global Justice

American Federation of Teachers

Amnesty International

The Brookings Institution

C-SPAN

Central Intelligence Agency

Delaware Nature Society

Jane Goodall Institute

National Public Radio

Philadelphia Eagles

Philadelphia Museum of Art

Sierra Club

Smithsonian Institution

U.S. Department of Commerce

The Washington Post

The Wildlife Society

XM Satellite Radio

MIDWEST

American Red Cross of Greater Chicago
Chicago International Film Festival
Coldwell Banker Real Estate
Fox Cable Networks
The Jerry Springer Show
Land O Lakes
Mall of America
The Minneapolis Institute of Arts
Missouri Botanical Garden
Planned Parenthood
SC Johnson

NEW YORK

ABC Carpet & Home
Bad Boy Worldwide Entertainment Group
Bertelsmann Media Worldwide
Brooklyn Academy of Music
Brooklyn Botanic Garden
Calvin Klein, Inc.
Carnegie Hall
Citigroup
Columbia Records
Condé Nast Publications
Con Edison
Christie's
DC Comics

Fox Searchlight Pictures
IMG
Lincoln Center for the Performing Arts
Liz Claiborne
The Metropolitan Museum of Art
MTV Networks (MTV, VH1, Comedy Central)
The New York Times
Sesame Workshop
SIRIUS Satellite Radio
Smith Barney
Tribeca Film Center
The Wall Street Journal

NEW ENGLAND

Appalachian Mountain Club
Boston Celtics
The Boston Globe
The Fleet Center
Grassroots International
World Fellowship Center
Xerox Corporation

ROCKIES

The Aspen Institute
Aspen Music Festival and School
Bravo! Vail Valley Music Festival
Breckenridge Outdoor Education Center

Colorado Historical Society
Dreamtime Festival
ManiaTV! Network

SOUTHEAST

Alabama Sports Festival
BDO Seidman, LLP
Birmingham Civil Rights Institute
Delta Airlines
Walt Disney World
Ladies Professional Golf Association
Little Rock Air Force Base
Orlando Magic
Relevant Media Group
Saks Inc.

SOUTHWEST

Georgia O'Keeffe Museum
Make-A-Wish Foundation
Outside magazine
Texas Instruments

WEST COAST

Amnesty International, USA
Apple Computer, Inc.
Berlex
Gap Inc.

Infinity Broadcasting Corporation
Mattel, Inc.
The Oregonian
Paramount Pictures
Teachers Without Borders
Warner Music Group
Wells Fargo

UNIQUE INTERNSHIPS

Andy Warhol Museum
Anheuser-Busch
Heineken
Mall of America

WEB SITES

http://intern.studyabroad.com
http://rtpnet.org/%7Eintintl/
www.careerbuilder.com
www.careernet.com
www.collegegrad.com/internships
www.internabroad.com
www.internshipprograms.com
www.internships.com
www.internships-usa.com
www.internweb.com
www.job-hunt.org/interns.shtml
www.monstertrak.monster.com/

www.usajobs.opm.gov
www.whitehouse.gov/government/wh-intern.html

REFERENCE BOOKS

Peterson's Internships 2006: Find the Right Internship for You

Vault Guide to Top Internships

The Internship Bible, 10th Edition (Princeton Review)

Best 109 Internships (Princeton Review)

Internships for Dummies

The Resume.com Guide to Writing Unbeatable Resumes

College Majors Handbook with Real Career Paths and Payoffs: The Actual Jobs, Earnings, and Trends for Graduates of 60 College Majors

JAMIE FEDORKO is a born and bred New Yorker. He attended Eugene Lang College and interned for *Paper* and *VIBE* magazines and *The McEnroe Show* on CNBC before writing *The Intern Files*. He has dreamed of becoming a writer for as long as he can remember. This is his first book.

BEFORE MUSIC GOES ANYWHERE ELSE, IT GRADUATES FROM mtvU.

NEW ARTISTS, VIDEOS AND CONCERT TOURS – IF IT'S MUSIC, WE'VE GOT IT. BUT THAT'S NOT ALL: STUDENT FILMS, KILLER INTERNSHIPS, JOB PREVIEWS, LIFE-CHANGING CONTESTS THAT JUMPSTART CAREERS, CAMPUS EVENTS LIKE THE TAILGATE TOUR AND VIDEO GAME TOUR. mtvU ENHANCES YOUR ENTIRE COLLEGE EXPERIENCE.

TUNE IN ALL SEMESTER LONG.

LIVE OFF CAMPUS? WATCH ONLINE WITH mtvU **Über** AT mtvU.COM